Practicing Feminist Mothering

practicing feminist mothering

FIONA JOY GREEN

ARBEITER RING PUBLISHING • WINNIPEG

Arbeiter Ring Publishing
201E-121 Osborne Street
Winnipeg, Manitoba
Canada R3L 1Y4
www.arbeiterring.com

Printed in Canada by Kromar Printing
Design by Relish Design Studio

MANITOBA ARTS COUNCIL
CONSEIL DES ARTS DU MANITOBA

Canada Council for the Arts — Conseil des Arts du Canada

Canadian Heritage — Patrimoine canadien

Manitoba

With assistance of the Manitoba Arts Council/Conseil des Arts du Manitoba.

We acknowledge the support of the Canada Council for our publishing program.

ARP acknowledges the financial support to our publishing activities of the Manitoba Arts Council/Conseil des Arts du Manitoba, Manitoba Culture, Heritage and Tourism, and the Government of Canada through the Canada Book Fund.

Arbeiter Ring Publishing acknowledges the support of the Province of Manitoba through the Book Publishing Tax Credit and the Book Publisher Marketing Assistance Program.

Printed on 100% recycled paper.

LIBRARY AND ARCHIVES CANADA CATALOGUING IN PUBLICATION

Green, Fiona J.
Practicing feminist mothering / Fiona Joy Green.

Includes bibliographical references and index.
ISBN 978-1-894037-54-9

1. Feminism. 2. Motherhood. 3. Child rearing.
4. Feminist theory. I. Title.

HG1155.G74 2011 306.874'3 C2011-906337-9

FSC
www.fsc.org
MIX
Paper from responsible sources
FSC® C103113

To my son Liam, who has taught me through his own brave and loving example how to live fully as oneself.

To Barry, my lifelong partner and father of Liam, who has so lovingly helped me in my feminist mothering.

ACKNOWLEDGMENTS

I am very grateful and indebted to the 16 mothers and the five daughters who so kindly gave of their time and shared their insight with me over the past dozen years as I engaged in the research project that informs this book. Without their generous participation, this book would not be possible.

I am especially thankful for my incredibly encouraging colleagues Roewan Crowe, Angela Failler, and Pauline Greenhill in the Department of Women's and Gender Studies at the University of Winnipeg, and to our former Department Assistant, Lou Lepine, for her ongoing support and for the many hours she worked transcribing my interviews with the mothers and daughters whose experiences appear in this book. I am thankful for the positive energy of Kim Hunter, the Events and Projects Coordinator for the Institute for Women's and Gender Studies, who buoyed my spirits many times during the last push of the book.

I am grateful for Peter Ives, Arbeiter Ring Publishing editorial collective member, whose engaging conversations over coffee, and thorough reading and insightful suggestions on the draft of this manuscript has made writing this book an empowering and positive experience. I also deeply appreciate Gina Wong for reading and reviewing this manuscript, and for her theory of matroreform that I draw upon and further develop in this work.

My research on feminist mothers and daughters was funded by a Research Development Initiative Grant from the Social Sciences Research Council of Canada. Several internal research and travel grants from the University of Winnipeg assisted some of the research and writing of the book, for which I am grateful.

While writing this book consumed two years of my life, my thinking about feminist mothering began twenty-three years ago with the birth of my son Liam. Over that time I have had the good fortune of sharing my ideas and engaging in discussions with various folks. Rozena Maart, who I first met at the University of York while we were in the MA Women's Studies program during the mid 1980s, has been a constant friend who, over the subsequent years, has joined me in telephone conversations to share our stories of mothering and critically think through the practical application of our feminism in our mothering. Andrea O'Reilly, founder of MIRCI (Motherhood Initiative for Research and Community Involvement, formerly known as Association for Research on Mothering), has been a tremendous influence in the development of my scholarship and champion of my work. As a feminist mother and maternal scholar, she understands the complexities of the praxis of feminist mothering and the challenges of being an academic researching and writing in this area. Without the work of Andrea O'Reilly, maternal theory and motherhood studies would not be the influential force it is today. I, along with many others, am extremely indebted to Andrea.

I am most deeply grateful for my own families of origin and of creation. To my parents Ed and Claire Green, who immigrated to Canada with my sister Jenny and me in 1967, thank you for teaching me to take risks and that I can be who I want to be, even when it has meant challenging you and being unpopular with others for my ideas and principles. To my incredible siblings Jenny Ayers, Diane Rothdram, and Ian Green, thank you for showing me how to be fully engaged in life in ways that are honest, accepting, and loving. And to my dear partner Barry Edginton, who has been at my side from the very beginning of this amazing journey of parenting and who has tirelessly supported my development as an academic and human being, thank you for your intelligence, patience, companionship and for knowing me so well. And to my dearest son Liam for whom I'm blessed each and every day, thank you for your love and compassion, for your passionate vision of life, and for your strength and commitment to be true to yourself.

INTRODUCTION

Affirming the Marginalized Voices of Feminist Mothers

For as long as I can remember, I have been a feminist. Although I didn't have the language to call myself "feminist" as a girl growing up in the 1960s and through my teens in the 1970s, I was certainly in tune with the unfairness I felt because I was "just a girl." I was easily angered when I saw other people, especially other girls, being ignored, bullied, or treated badly. I was sure of my agency and believed I had the right to speak up against such injustices for myself and for others. My quick temper soon became my trademark, and I was known as a tough and feisty tomboy who would go to battle with anyone, over anything, at any time, for whatever I thought was unfair. I felt powerful and completely justified in challenging people who treated me, and others, unfairly.

When I entered university in the mid 1980s, having worked and travelled in the five years since graduating from high school, I soon learned that my understanding of the world was supported by my undergraduate studies in the areas of Anthropology and Sociology. I learned of theorists who viewed the situation and position of girls and women in similar ways; I was introduced to, and was soon using, a new vocabulary that helped name and explain my gendered experiences in the world. I thrived on knowing that I was becoming part of a collective of women that had a herstory of experience, knowledge, and analysis that explained the world in ways that made sense to me and offered practical ways of questioning, contesting, and disrupting the social system named patriarchy that perpetuated this unbalanced and indefensible situation.

During those first few years at university while in my early twenties I was generally critical of men, yet I fell in love with and married my husband. I finished my BA, and while my spouse was on sabbatical as a visiting scholar in England, I followed my interest in feminism and undertook an MA in Women's Studies. After attending an international homebirth conference in London shortly after we first arrived in the UK, and recognizing that homebirths were not legal or supported in Manitoba at that time, we tried to conceive. We were very fortunate, and I successfully birthed our son in England, a month after I handed in my thesis *The Development of a Mother-Centred Model of Childbirth*.

My MA research and ever-developing feminist consciousness profoundly influenced my understanding of the medicalization of pregnancy and its repercussions for women. It also strengthened my ability to make sense of my own pregnancy and birthing experience. Rather than being a passive patient, I was an active participant exercising agency with medical professionals regarding medical decisions about my body and fetus throughout my pregnancy, when I underwent an emergency caesarean section in hospital, and during my post surgery recovery.

The process of researching, writing, birthing my son and becoming a mother enabled me to make meaningful connections among my life experiences, feminist analysis, and theorizing. For example, my partner and I chose to hyphenate our son's last name to honour both his maternal and paternal ancestry. Like other feminist mothers, I enacted my feminism by refusing to support and reproduce the patriarchal practice of naming children solely after their paternal family line. Just as I have kept my "maiden" or given name upon getting married to demonstrate my independent identity apart from my husband and my continuing connection to my (albeit patrilineal) heritage, our son's name illustrates his connection to both of his parents, not just to his father.

As our son developed, I realized for the first time that males, just as females, are expected to conform to socially prescribed gender-specific stereotypes. When I was a girl, teenager, and young woman, I felt pressure to behave in gender-specific ways, and as a university student, I came to understand how the social construction of female identity both fosters subjugation and sustains patriarchal power. I was not, however, cognizant of similar pressure placed on boys until I experienced, firsthand, the insistence by others that my son conform to socially sanctioned, accepted, and rewarded standards of "masculinity." The type of clothing he wore, toys he played with, activities he was involved in, and the ways in which he interacted with people were all restricted by notions of who boys should/not be and what boys should/not be doing. I quickly recognized how my feminism had helped me interpret the effects of sexism and misogyny in the lives of girls and women but had not helped me to recognize the influence of sexism, misogyny, and patriarchal gender roles on boys and men.

I observed the pressure my son was under to conform to gender stereotypes as a five-year-old kindergarten student in an independent school. Due to the many conversations I had about my son's unconventional appearance with teachers, parents, and students that year, I was acutely aware of the confusion and unease people had with my son's gender presentation. My most vivid memory of that time is of an exchange I had with the mother of a child in my son's class. As we waited to pick our children up after school she questioned why my "daughter," who had shoulder-length hair sporting a colourful hair wrap, was wearing the standard shirt and short uniform for boys. When I explained that the child she assumed was my daughter was my son, she responded with the comment, "Oh!

But she's—I mean he's—so pretty." Shortly after this revelation she queried the school's policy regarding the "uniform and dress code." The mother's tactic of turning our conversation to official school policy regarding boys' hair and dress suggested to me that she considered my son's hair length and style inappropriate and that I should have it cut in a fashion more fitting for a boy. It also suggested to me that she thought the school should ensure that my son comply with the stereotypical mainstream image of boys if I would not voluntarily do so. Although the beginning of our conversation had started out with a fairly gentle inquiry about my son's appearance, it quickly shifted to a discussion of how the school should regulate my decisions as a mother. Since I had allowed—or even encouraged—my son to grow and decorate his hair in a style presumed only suitable for girls, she felt free to question my decisions and abilities as a mother.

This interaction, along with others regarding my son's appearance by people inside and outside the school system in those early years, made me think more deeply about the expectations placed on me as a mother. Before becoming a mother I knew I would feel some pressure to raise my child according to social expectations, yet I had not fully understood, nor imagined, the degree to which those expectations included replicating and promoting patriarchal values and practices. I was not prepared for the intense social surveillance and resulting pressures to raise my son in ways that duplicated patriarchal notions of masculinity. I now saw and understood that mothers were required to pass patriarchal perspectives, values, and behaviours on to their children, and I felt the scrutinizing gaze and consequential disapproval that mothers met, especially from other mothers, when they didn't comply.

These revelations—that the socialization and development of males are influenced by patriarchy and that mothers are strongly encouraged to reproduce and advocate patriarchal expectations—now appear naïve. They did, however, demonstrate how my feminist analysis was limited and how mothering could broaden my knowledge, understanding, and practice of feminism. As in other areas of my life, mothering is a site where personal action is political and where general societal values are reflected in personal experience. I saw how mothering had become a location where my feminist activism could question and challenge, rather than support and replicate, patriarchy. By consciously choosing to support my son's decision to have longer hair, rather than forcing him to cut it to conform to a style considered suitable for boys, I exposed, troubled, and contradicted the patriarchal expectation that I would reproduce a "masculine" boy in the way patriarchy deemed acceptable. In refusing to reproduce this particular patriarchal expectation placed on me as a mother, I also offered an alternative vision and practice of mothering, parenting, and masculinity.[1]

Realizing that mothering had become a site of feminist political activism for me, I wondered if other feminist mothers also found mothering to be a place where they practiced their feminism. I was curious about how they understood feminism, what they thought of motherhood and if their feminism and mothering influenced each other. More specifically, I was interested in exploring if, and how, feminist mothers distinguish between their potential power as mothers and the idealized concepts and practices of motherhood that attempt to suppress women's power suggested by feminist maternal scholar Adrienne Rich.[2]

Outlining my experience here is not meant to claim an essentialized identity of a feminist mother nor an authoritative voice on feminist mothering. Rather I share this story to offer a point of entry into the research and writing process, to make visible my social location, and to remain aware of the ways in which my personal history may show up in the trajectories of my own knowledge and ignorance.

These personal revelations and questions about the experiences of other feminist mothers not only prompted me to investigate the interconnections between feminism and mothering in my PhD research and dissertation, they also inspired my further thinking addressed in more recent publications.[3] This book, *Practicing Feminist Mothering*, continues my ongoing inquiry into the dynamic juncture between feminism and mothering by further exploring the complex and evolving practices of feminist mothering that dispute and counteract the myths surrounding contemporary patriarchal motherhood. It explores how feminist mothering can actively empower women and children to create social change, and provides new insights into understanding the interconnections between feminism and mothering in the lives of feminist mothers and their children.[4] It also reveals ways in which we might think more critically and creatively about motherhood, mothering, and parenting, and about feminism and feminist mothering.

I am influenced by the writings of Patricia Hill Collins (1987; 1994; 2000) and Maureen Reddy (1994) that theorize the complexities of race and racism in mothering, by the work of Katherine Arnup (1988; 1989), Julie Ainslie and Kathryn Feltey (1992), the Boston Lesbian Psychologies Collective (1987), Rachel Epstein (2010), and Sandra Pollack and Jeanne Vaughn (1987) that address the multifaceted realities of queer parenting, along with the work of Heather Kuttai (2010) and Aimee Mullins (2005) who speak to the challenges and lessons of pregnancy, mothering, and child care with a disability. I am greatly influenced by the observation of American feminist, poet, mother, and scholar, Adrienne Rich (1986) that motherhood is both an individual experience and a social institution, and by her proposition that we need to consider how mothers understand and engage motherhood. These authors speak to the importance of noticing and questioning how various social locations of mothers influence the experiences of motherhood and mothering, and like them, I believe that a women-centred approach that honours the voices and experiences of women is best suited to researching and understanding the complexities of women's life experiences.

I also agree with feminist theorists such as Bianca Jagger (2009), Chandra Mohanty (1991; 1991a; 2003), Gayatri Spivak (1996), and Minh-ha Trinh (1986) that there is not a single, pure, essential woman's experience out of which universal analytical categories can be developed, but rather, there are multiple experiences and understandings of women's realities. And just as the meaning of feminism is not static nor monolithic but instead multi-dimensional, fluid, and ever-changing because feminisms are created by folks who are analyzing the oppression of themselves and others with the purpose of social change, the meaning and experiences of feminist mothering are akin to a matrix that is in constant motion over time and circumstance.

Documenting and analyzing the diversity of women's experiences, which often consist of, but are not limited to, the socially prescribed and maintained categories of ability, age, class, ethnicity, gender, geographic location, race, religion, sex, sexuality, and sexual orientation, is vital to building theoretical understandings of gender that include a variety of meanings and interpretations that inform their experiences as feminist mothers.

A large portion of *Practicing Feminist Mothering* draws upon and explores the self-reported parenting practices of sixteen self-identified feminist mothers over fifteen or more years, and the insights that five of their adult female children have regarding the influence of their mothers' feminist parenting in their own lives, and on their ideas and practices of feminism and mothering. Much of this research into the lived experiences of feminist mothers and their daughters engages a hybrid methodological approach that incorporates elements of three methodologies: 1) Feminist methodologies address the life experiences of people, most often women, who continue to be considered peripheral to academic research and society by placing them as active participants at the centre of both inquiry and analysis;[5] 2) Research from the margins advocates ways for researchers to gather, make sense of, and act responsibly with information that is shared with them by individuals who experience social injustice, inequality, and exploitation in ways that honour their voices, experiences, and knowledge;[6] and 3) Grounded Theory uses a systematic set of procedures to develop an inductively derived theory about a phenomenon with the purpose to build theory that is faithful to and illuminates the area under study.[7]

This hybrid methodological approach that uses one-on-one, intensive interviews with feminist mothers and some of their adult daughters about their subjective knowledge regarding their feminisms and their experiences of feminist mothering highlights, acknowledges, and affirms the ways in which mothers practice their feminism through their mothering and how their daughters understand their mother's feminist parenting.[8] The process of keeping their knowledge central to the research helps ensure that the themes within the interviews generate an analytical framework that contributes to developing understandings and meanings of embodied feminisms within this moving and ever-changing milieu. Since I am particularly interested in what can be learned about feminism, mothering, and activism from feminist mothers and their relationships with their children, which have been overlooked, ignored, or silenced in the past, considerable attention is paid to how feminist mothers and their adult female children experience the interconnection of feminism and mothering in their lives, and to the ongoing work of feminist praxis, feminist activism, feminist matroreform, and feminist motherlines.

Chapter One "The Legacy of Feminism and Motherhood" reviews and contextualizes Western feminist theorizing and writing about motherhood over the past fifty years since the dawn of the second wave of feminism in the late 1960s. This initial chapter speaks to some of the general trends of feminist thinking around motherhood and mothering and illustrates how motherhood and mothering have been a concern for feminists over time. It also demonstrates how this rich feminist discourse on mothering and motherhood continues to grow. Drawing on the sometimes contradictory analysis of others and on my own reading and thinking, I review some of the trends of past feminist writing on motherhood and provide some insight into the social and political milieu of the time when the feminist mothers featured in this book developed their understanding of feminism and motherhood and practiced their feminist mothering.

The second chapter, "The Praxis of Feminist Mothering," explores the ways in which self-identified feminist mothers understand feminism, mothering, and motherhood and how this convergence underpins their conscious practice of feminist mothering. Regardless of whether they began parenting as feminists, mothered as feminists once they became parents, or parented with a partner, alone, or in a hybrid situation, these feminist mothers purposefully choose to parent in ways that are informed by and embody their feminism. By understanding how mothering is a feminist and a political act, we learn how feminist mothering is a site of feminist praxis for some and how feminism provides these particular women with a worldview that allows them to critically question the concepts and expectations associated with motherhood, and to invent and live their feminism through their parenting. The purpose is not to prescribe an idealized approach to feminist mothering for others to replicate, but rather to explain some ways in which particular self-identified feminist mothers have brought together their feminism and mothering.

"Matroreform: Breaking the Rules of Motherhood" is the title of Chapter Three, which looks more closely at the complicated positioning of feminist mothers and the ways in which they navigate societal and internalized expectations of motherhood and their own understandings of feminism and parenting. Attention is given to how mothers resist the damaging elements of the institution and ideology of motherhood and how they create space to parent in ways that respect their own experience and knowledge. The chapter critically examines how feminist mothers understand, trouble, and oppose the dynamics of power and control in mother/child relationships, and concludes by arguing that feminist mothers engage in matroreform through the conscious process of (re)claiming mothering power by establishing alternative rules and practicing different customs to those previously prescribed by others.[9]

Chapter Four, "Creating Feminist Motherlines: Feminist Mothers and their Daughters," examines the experiences and reflections of feminist mothering from the perspectives of five adult daughters of four feminist mothers. Of particular interest is how the daughters perceive their mother's feminism and its influences on their upbringing, and how their own understanding of feminism and mothering is related to their identities and lives. These reflections provide insight into how feminist motherlines are being created by both mothers and daughters, and how, through their joint reflective understandings of their life experiences as mothers and daughters, they understand and contest patriarchal norms of motherhood to empower themselves by living their lives with authority, agency, and autonomy.[10]

The volume ends with a "Conclusion" that provides an overview of the main arguments and findings of the book and suggests some ways in which we might work to recognize the complexities of the praxis of feminist mothering, while maintaining a focus on the larger social context and the importance of matroreform and feminist motherliness. By exploring the sustained practices of child rearing used by particular feminist mothers over time and the influences they have had on their adult children, the possibilities for social change and new ways of theorizing and practicing feminism and mothering become clearer.

CHAPTER I

The Legacy of Feminism and Motherhood

> "Mothers need feminism just as urgently as feminism needs to think about the many social problems that face mothers."[11]

> "Feminists need to listen to the experiences of mothers and... mothers, in turn, need feminism."[12]

Mothering and motherhood have been "critical themes for feminists" in North America since the second wave of feminism when women demanded they had the right to shape their own destinies.[13] Since then, motherhood and mothering have also been "the fulcrum of feminist concern" in American black feminist thought, in lesbian and queer theorizing, in writings about gender and disability, in Indigenous women's writing and organizing, and in other North American countercultural discourses.[14]

It seems highly appropriate, given the fairly recent passing of three prominent feminist maternal scholars—Sara Ruddick (1935–2011), Marilyn French (1929–2009), and Betty Friedan (1921–2006)—that, in this first chapter, I review various currents of feminist thinking and attitudes towards motherhood, mothering, and mothers since the late 1960s, when feminism resurfaced after a dearth of interest in women's rights during the inter- and post war years in 20th century North America. I focus primarily on the twenty years spanning the 1970s through the 1990s, which encapsulates the latter part of the second wave of feminism from the late 1960s to the late 1980s, and the twenty years at the beginning of the third wave of feminism from the early 1990s to 2010 because the understandings and practices of feminism and mothering of the women featured in this book were developed and carried out during this timeframe.[15] Further discussion about the women featured in this book is provided in Chapters Two, Three, and Four. This initial chapter speaks to the general trends of feminist theorizing around motherhood and mothering within this selected period to illustrate how motherhood and mothering have been a concern for feminists over time and to demonstrate how this rich feminist discourse on mothering and motherhood continues to grow. Drawing on the sometimes contradictory analysis of others and on my own reading and thinking, I offer a limited review of some of the trends of past feminist writing on motherhood, which provides a brief social context of the time the feminist mothers developed their understanding of feminism and motherhood and how they practiced their feminist mothering.[16]

The First Half of the Second Wave of Feminism: Late 1960s through the 1970s

For many feminists writing and organizing in the late 1960s and the 1970s, everything surrounding the question of women and mothers appeared to be a product of patriarchy,[17] which was understood as the socially accepted and supported rule of men over women and children through greater status, wealth, and power.[18] Motherhood, which was understood to be a social arrangement of roles and responsibilities given primarily to women who were without power to define and determine mothering based on their own experiences, was viewed by many as a particular patriarchal trap that helped to maintain a sex/gender hierarchy that disadvantaged girls and women.[19] The role of motherhood was also understood to buttress hierarchies of class and race. For instance, Anna Davin wrote an article in 1978 examining the role of imperialism in developing the expectations associated with the mandatory position of mothering for women in Britain at the turn of the 20th century and beyond.

She also shows the ways in which imperialism and patriarchy have informed an ideology of motherhood for the Western world ever since.[20] Motherhood was therefore identified as, and criticized for, being a patriarchal institution that resulted in many social and psychological problems for women.[21]

Yet, many feminists at that time engaged in feminist consciousness-raising groups where they spoke honestly and passionately about their lived experiences and began to draw the connection between those experiences and the way in which society was structured to favour men over women. They saw how their experiences in personal and intimate relationships, their experiences as students and employees, and their experiences as members of civil rights and student activist groups were similar because of their shared gender identity as women. Many feminists came to understand the personal to be political and that the work of mothering, which was done in the privacy of women's homes, was "a form of politics, a social act that needed social recognition."[22]

Feminist consciousness during the early years of the second wave of feminism generally rejected patriarchal defined maternity, which was evident in women's personal beliefs and in feminist writings of the time. For instance, *The Feminine Mystique,* written by American feminist, mother, and journalist Betty Friedan in 1963, names marriage and motherhood as primary sources of women's unhappiness and depression. Friedan identified "the problem with no name" as a sense of dissatisfaction that many middle-class American women felt with their lives, and explained the reason for the feeling was being limited by the narrow and restrictive roles of wives and mothers. She also explained how and why women had a right to expect more when they dared to ask themselves the question: "Is this all I can expect as a woman?"

The Second Sex written by French existentialist philosopher Simone de Beauvoir, and translated into English in 1972, critiques women's maternity within patriarchy and argues that "the experience of maternity [cannot be understood] when the mother's subjectivity is not recognized and when women are given no concrete choices or opportunities in the world."[23] And American feminist Shulamith Firestone's controversial and utopian *The Dialectic of Sex: The Case for Feminist Revolution* (1970) argues that women's biologically determined positions as breeders and child care providers are the source of gender inequality and that human reproduction through the nonjudgmental widespread use of abortion and contraception, the practice of cybernectics in laboratories, and state-supported child rearing would free women from the oppressive physical and physiological role of motherhood.[24] Although often accused of being "a mother-hating book" that is "strangely blind" about motherhood, a careful read of this text calls for feminists to "smash patriarchy, not mothers" and "to imagine a responsibility to kids which is not biological."[25] Firestone, like Friedan and de Beauvoir, identifies the social response to women's reproductive capacities and abilities, rather than women, to be the prime barrier to women's equality.[26] Yet, women's emancipation during this time is nevertheless generally viewed as a move away from motherhood.

The best-selling novel *The Woman's Room* (1978) written by American feminist Marilyn French crystallized "a mood of fury and despair that some women felt about men, and some mothers felt about the fathers of their children" when it suggested that "women may be better off alone, unhappy perhaps, but free."[27] Many mothers during this era attempted to find freedom from motherhood and its associated oppressions, much like many feminist women in general tried to free themselves from all patriarchal institutions (such as the church, the state, and the economy) and their associated oppressions.[28] This radical and harsh feminist self-questioning about motherhood during the first half of the second wave of feminism, while often misread as an attack on mothers and housewives and a complete disregard for motherhood, was perhaps at least a simplistic analysis of the complex reality of motherhood and mothering within patriarchal societies.[29]

The above noted authors, like many other equality feminists of the time who viewed women and men as equals, were struggling to gain equal access for women in existing institutions and believed that women's advances could only be obtained outside of the family. They saw themselves as breaking away from their mothers' lives and primarily identified themselves as "daughters celebrating sisterhood" with other women.[30] The metaphor of "sisterhood" was used during the early years of the second wave to offer an alternative to motherhood or daughterhood, and to describe a feminine model and ideal of relations whereby women had connections with each other outside the mother/daughter paradigm and with men outside the heteronormative wife/mother identity.[31] Unfortunately, one of the consequences of this strategy was that "the sisterly focus led many early second wave feminists to either abandon motherhood entirely, or, at best, make motherhood secondary, even for women who actually had children."[32]

Part of the struggle for feminists who were mothers during this time was that their voices were often unheard, unwelcomed, or misunderstood within feminist circles. American feminist, writer, and mother Robin Morgan, for example, notes the pressure she felt as a feminist to rebel against motherhood rather than combine her own identity as a mother with her feminist politics.[33] She believes her discomfort around and reluctance to declare her identity and experience as a mother during the 1970s was because feminism generally viewed motherhood as intrinsically connected with the reproduction of patriarchy and, therefore, implicated her as a mother.

Feminist mother and professor of French and Comparative Literature Marianne Hirsch speaks of an "unbridgeable maternal divide" she experiences during the late 1970s, between mothers and non-mothers who belonged to a group of friendly feminist academics who came together to find support as they struggled with institutional and personal concerns.[34] Hirsch believes the split occurred in this group because both factions of women had much invested in the decisions they had made about being mothers or not, and felt powerless for different reasons; mothers due to their daily responsibilities for their children and motherwork and non-mothers for their complicated ambivalences about mothering and the social and familial pressures they experienced as women without children.[35]

Unfortunately, writings about mothers and motherhood during the second wave often universalized the experience of mothering based on stereotypes and assumptions about the lives of white, middle-class, able-bodied heterosexual women living in the Western world, and as a result, added to the complicated and misunderstood experiences of mothering and motherhood.[36] Early exceptions to this trend include Toni Morrison's novel *Sula* (1973) and Alice Walker's short story "Everyday Use" (1973) because they focus upon the experiences of African American mothers who are angry, encourage insight into the complexities of maternal experiences, and illustrate the significance of diverse maternal subjectivities. These African American authors pushed readers to think about why it is so difficult to hear maternal rage and to accept a range of experiences from women as mothers.[37] Their writings helped articulate and support the argument "It is impossible to conclude that mothers *act* in any one way, or that their *actions* have enough in common to constitute a *practice*."[38]

Jessie Bernard's *The Future of Motherhood* (1974) is one of the first publications to investigate motherhood as a social institution rather than as a fact of nature. She argues motherhood is a role women learn through cultural imperatives—such as family, religion, and education—and a role that is profoundly changed by factors such as women's increased labour force participation, decreasing birthrates, and the occurrence of and isolation within the nuclear family.[39]

American feminist, poet, theorist, and mother Adrienne Rich developed this argument further two years later in *Of Woman*

Born: Motherhood as Experience and Institution (1976) in which she makes the critical distinction between the patriarchal institution of motherhood and women's experiences of mothering which, while informed by the oppressive institution of motherhood, are not completely controlled by it. Mothers are seen as persons/subjects in their own right who, as sisters in feminism, have agency to challenge, create, and resist the restrictive institution of motherhood from within.[40] The wide range of emotional responses to the work of mothering, a mother's relationships with her children, and the experience of child rearing within the institution of motherhood are openly addressed in *Of Woman Born*.

Rich also criticized the general feminist response of daughters rejecting their mothers due to "matrophobia"—the fear of becoming one's mother—and speculated that motherhood, the organization of the work of mothering prescribed almost solely to women as mothers, is the reason for this fear and is thus in need of a radical transformation.[41] She claimed that the proscribed ways in which motherwork is to be undertaken by women is the source of the problem, not the inherent worth of mothers.

Bernard and Rich were instrumental in shifting feminist thinking around the key distinction between the political conditions that structure women's lives, and the personal experiences and realities of mothers living within those socially constructed and enforced institutions and locations. The work of Rich, in particular, helped to shatter the previous taboo of not honouring women's own honest descriptions of the emotional complexity of mothering and encouraged others to explore their genuine experiences of mothering. In addition, Carrie Carmichael wrote the first instructional book to help feminists raise their children in non-sexist ways and offered concrete examples of how some feminist mothers were living their feminist politics through their mothering in her 1977 book *Non-Sexist Childraising*.

These and other valuable works addressing some of the personal experiences of mothering corresponded with a general change in North American feminist thinking during the late 1970s and early 1980s from a philosophy and politic of "equality feminism" to one of "difference feminism" that attended to the specific experiences, knowledge/s and voices of women and pressured institutions to transform in ways that would accommodate the specific needs of women.[42] The larger force of the feminist movement and organizing fostered the establishment of Women's Studies courses, programs, and departments in universities across the continent, although they were often marginalized within and struggled to be fully accepted within and outside these educational institutions.[43]

The Second Half of the Second Wave: Moving into and through the 1980s

A number of texts written by feminists during the late 1970s and 1980s were influenced by object-relations psychoanalytic theory or by post-structuralism in relation to the development of the mother/child bond.[44] Carol Gilligan's publication of *In a Different Voice* in 1982, for instance, offered a different ethical model, one based on the development of girls through adolescence that emphasized satisfying human relationships premised upon connection, rather than a moral ethic based upon individuation and separation developed from studying males.[45]

All authors speak, in some degree, to the significance of the mother/daughter relationship and to the point that "every woman extends backwards into her mother and forwards into her daughter."[46] Their work generally reframed understandings of this primary relationship mostly from the perspective of the child,[47] and addressed the difficulty, as noted by Nancy Chodorow and Susan Contratto (1982), some previous feminists had during this period of speaking in a maternal voice due to their general ambivalence about power and authority, to their particular fear of their maternal anger with maternal powerlessness, and to their continued perception from the previous decade that mothering is a patriarchal construction or a form of collusion with patriarchy.[48]

Building on the work of Bernard (1974; 1976), Chodorow (1978), Flax (1978) and Rich (1976), feminists began to recognize the importance of a theory that links the most private family structures—including the work of mothering—to social, economic, and political structures. For example, "Chodorow and Dinnerstein perceived shared parenting in early infancy as the most important challenge to patriarchal rule, as the only way to challenge the severely skewed 'sexual arrangements' in which we live, [and as] the only way to make us 'fully human.'"[49] Others began to write using a maternal feminist voice to address the mother/child relationship from the lived experiences and perspective of the mother and reflect upon the pain and frustration of maternal experience. Adrienne Rich's *Of Woman Born* (1976) and Jane Lazarre's *The Mother Knot* (1976), like the previously mentioned works of Morrison and Walker, are among the first to address issues of separation, autonomy, and power relations within motherhood from the perspectives of mothers.[50] The two 1978 publications of Michelle Wallace's *Black Macho and the Myth of Super-Woman* and Rachel DuPlessis' special motherhood issue of *Feminist Studies* also attempt to pry mothering experiences away from the patriarchal institution of motherhood.[51]

Sara Ruddick's journal article "Maternal Thinking," first published in the summer of 1980, offered readers, feminists, and mothers a look into the practical realities of the work involved in mothering. By concentrating on "what mothers do rather than on what they are," Ruddick argued that mothering is not an innate ability in women but rather a social construct.[52] This new feminist approach explored and analyzed the practices and intellectual disciplines involved in rearing children and concluded that men and non-biological mothers can successfully practice mothering because "'maternal' is a social and not a biological category."[53] For Ruddick, "mothers are people who see children as 'demanding' protection, nurturance and training" and who "respond to children's demands with care and respect rather than indifference or assault."[54] Fortunately, the earlier resistance to listening to and honouring maternal voices began to fade by the end of the 1980s with these publications and a shift in understanding and analysis of mothering and motherhood.

Writings in the 1980s by American Black feminists, such as Patricia Hill Collins (1987; 1989), Bonnie Thornton Dill (1988), Marjorie Hill (1987), bell hooks (1984), Alice Walker (1983), and the 1981 edited collection *This Bridge Called My Back: Writings by Radical Women of Color,* pushed colonialism and racism to the surface of feminist analysis regarding motherhood, daughterhood, and parenting. By speaking to the resistant and complex relationships between African American mothers and daughters living within racist America and how mothers of colour have parented throughout history under conditions different from those of White or Euro-American mothers, the authors drew attention to the need for feminist theorizing to be local and multivocal; to cross boundaries of difference, whether due to race/ethnicity, class, sexual orientation, or parenting; and to build allied coalitions.[55]

Other writers addressed the ways in which mythologies, ideologies and cultural meanings of motherhood have been developed, perpetuated, and enforced over time.[56] In 1987 the history of the development and the ideal of the "good mother" are explored by Katherine Gieve in "Rethinking Feminist Attitudes towards Motherhood" and by Yvonne Schutz in *The Good Mother: The History of the Normative Model* to begin what would become a familiar practice of reviewing and critiquing feminist thinking about motherhood in the next decade.

Many of these significant feminist writings were published when Republican Ronald Reagan was President of the United

States from 1981–1989, with George Bush as Vice-President (and soon to be President from 1989–1993). During this period, the Republican Party pushed "family values" in the US, which included promoting heterosexual "traditional marriage," adoption and abstinence, rewarding a traditional role for women in the family through income tax and other measures, while also opposing sex outside of conventional marriage and disputing feminist advances in reproductive choice by opposing the legalization of abortion and sex education promoting safer sex. Reaganomics, also known as supply-side or trickle-down economics, was rampant in the US; the Republican government reduced government spending and regulation, reduced income tax and capital gains tax, and controlled the money supply in an effort to reduce inflation.[57]

Brian Mulroney, the leader of the Progressive Conservative Party of Canada and the Canadian Prime Minister from 1984 to 1993, found a friend in President Reagan, and pushed a policy and philosophy of neo-conservatism that viewed the marketplace as the best producer of economic activity and prosperity and the best distributor of goods and services. This approach objected to and, thus, limited government intervention in the workings of the marketplace and encouraged citizens to assume a greater responsibility for their individual well-being. Mulroney was committed to closer relations with the United States and the national leaders agreed on a $7 billion overhaul of the North American Aerospace Defense Command (NORAD) in March 1985 and the Canada-US Free Trade Agreement in October 1987.[58]

Like England's Prime Minister, Margaret Thatcher, Mulroney sold a number of state-owned companies and withdrew financial support from a number of women's organizations. Feminists during this time were more marginalized by the federal government than before and suffered great financial hardship with the cessation of funding to feminist organizations, research and projects.[59] Although not anti-feminist to the extent of Reagan and the Republicans in the US, Mulroney and his Conservative Party nevertheless sought to reverse a range of policies they claimed were the result of feminist "special interest groups."[60] Canadian feminist organizations and individuals were outraged by the cut in government funding to their programs, the limitations placed on their access to national policy discussions and processes, and the sympathy the government showed the anti-feminist, anti-abortion, pro-family organization REAL Women (Realistic, Equal, Active, for Life).[61] A significant political commitment and push for "family values" in Canada began in the late 1980s and early 1990s, with the formation of the Reform Party of Canada (1987–2000), which later became the Canadian Reform Conservative Alliance Party, more commonly known as the Alliance Party, in 2000.[62]

During this neo-conservative era, difference feminism was assessed by some feminist critics as being too focused on gender and, thus, ignoring other important areas of difference among women, such as race/ethnicty, class, economic status, and sexual orientation. Difference feminism was also criticized for "essentializing women's experience," which both flattened out the richness and complexity of women's realities and knowledge and was often read as "returning women to the destiny of their anatomy," specifically in relation to mothering.[63] By being "unable to envision a meaningful life for women outside of motherhood," some feminists experienced difference feminism as alienating and "even 'violent' in its exclusionary power," often criticizing it for being too narrow to make any significant lasting social change.[64] American feminist theorist and mother Marianne Hirsch argues that a "mother inclusive feminism" that recognized and acknowledged the vast differences among mothers and their experiences due to historical, cultural, and social conditions, while also resisting the projection and idealization of motherhood, was still lacking at the end of the second wave of feminism.

Although books such as *The Second Stage* by Betty Friedan (1981), *A Lesser Life: The Myth of Women's Liberation in*

America (1986) by Silvia Ann Hewlett, *The Sacred Bond: The Legacy of Baby M* by Phyllis Chesler (1988), and *The Second Shift* by Arlie Hochschild (1989) were published during the 1980s, they addressed a limited range of mothering experiences and contexts by mostly addressing the middle-class experience of mothers and the ways in which they were buried as autonomous people within the family due to the responsibility and the reality of doing most of the domestic work without support or recognition of losing wealth and financial security through no-fault divorce, and of losing children through homophobic laws and legislation that punished lesbian and queer mothers.[65]

During the latter 1980s and well into the 1990s, feminism in general experienced a backlash for the gains made in the 1970s and early 1980s, and mothers, in particular, were a large target both within and outside feminism.[66] Liberal feminism continued to challenge the dominant ideology of motherhood, utilizing a vocabulary of rights, responsibilities, justice, equity, empowerment, and identity to push the argument that mothers are persons with individual and social rights.[67] While feminist writing on motherhood during the mid 1980s and 1990s continued to address issues such as sex, hunger, poverty, pornography, art, power, and self-esteem, it appeared to "soften its approach to motherhood,"[68] partly because feminists were generally having trouble distinguishing motherhood as an all-encompassing duty from mothering that is only one of many possible elements in a woman's life.[69] This narrow approach may have been persistent because "feminism's great works of the past have always been a form of writing against the assumption that motherhood is all that women can do."[70]

Since the politics of the second wave built upon the older feminist view that motherhood was an essentially restricting location and problem that needed solving, it often left women's experiences of mothering and motherhood unexpressed.[71] Furthermore, governments in North America and England alike were doing and saying little about working women. Women who had wanted children and had put off child rearing for their careers, and mothers who had assumed their careers would be easy to pick up again once they rejoined the labour force, were equally struggling to find support.[72] Not only was the work of mothering and the responsibilities for caring for others still assigned to women, women continued to find it difficult to speak to each other about their circumstances. When women did speak, they were not generally heard outside the bounds of feminism and their unhappy feelings about motherhood were often experienced by mothers as their own personal failings rather than the responsibility of a sexist and patriarchal social structure.[73] Furthermore, earlier feminist approaches and strategies of the 1970s had become restrained by the feminist backlash of the 1980s, leaving mainstream feminism hesitant to challenge the system for its repressive organization of child rearing that it was still trying to join.[74]

The mid 1980s also witnessed a trend whereby some middle-class career women wanted to be full-time stay-at-home mothers. Some employers responded by developing what became known as the "Mommy Track": employment options that offered flexible working hours yet restricted opportunities for career advancement to female employees who were, or wanted to become, mothers. This new career path choice for a few middle-class women may have become a viable alternative to the ways in which mothering, fathering, and parenting could be practiced if all women, as well as men and fathers, were allowed to equally participate in the "mommy track."[75]

Multiple maternal voices still needed to be included and respected in feminist theorizing and activism in ways that recognized that mothering is not the sole goal for women, that spoke positively of women who are not mothers, that did not foster pro-natalism, and that did not sentimentalize and/or blame mothers.[76] By speaking as a survivor and empowered woman who claims her maternal experience and maternal subjectivity, African American author Toni Morrison again modelled the kind of conversations feminists needed to be having about the divergent experiences of women within oppressive institutions of patriarchy, slavery, and capitalism in *Beloved*.[77] Her maternal voice of resistance within this 1987 novel drew attention to the complex configurations and shapes of maternal knowledge, experience, and subjectivity. Feminists during this period slowly recognized the importance of affiliations, as well as the significance of particularity and distinction among maternal contexts and experiences.[78]

Embarking on a feminist project that is inclusive of mothers and their experiences requires space and respect for a cacophony of voices and understandings of mothering that counter the narrow cultural stereotypes and oppositional positionings of mothers and daughters that reflects the matrophobia, first identified by Rich, that exists both in individual relationships between daughters and mothers, and within feminism and society at large.[79]

As the end of the second wave dissipated and the third wave began, feminism needed to develop a perspective of motherhood and mothering—of which this book is a part—that detailed and sympathized with the lives and experiences of mothers to counter the over-simplistic assumptions about motherhood, what mothers did and how they should be mothering that had been rooted in earlier feminist theorizing and writing.

Third Wave Feminism of the early 1990s to 2010

The 1990s was a time of reflection for feminists, in part because of the current backlash they were experiencing, and in part because it had been a quarter century since the inception of the second wave. Some North American feminists, like Canadian academics Sharon Abby and Andrea O'Reilly (1998), Canadian sociologist Roberta Hamilton (1990), American novelist Maureen Freely (1995), American activist Ann Snitow (1992), American professor of comparative literature Diana Taylor (1997), and American historian Lauri Umansky (1996) took the opportunity at this significant historical moment to review the relationship between feminism and mothering by charting and reflecting upon the ways in which some believed motherhood to be at odds with feminism, while others understood there to be an ongoing and changing connection between the two.

Feminist scholars and theorists also examined the role that medical, scientific, and education professions had in developing and perpetuating the ideology of motherhood and instructing mothers how to be "good mothers" through their work as general physicians, psychiatrists, scientists, teachers, and child-rearing experts. Such titles in this area of research include "Constructing Mothers: Scientific Motherhood in the Nineteenth and Twentieth Centuries (Apple, 1995), *Women, Motherhood and Child Rearing* (Richardson, 1993), and "'Motherhood Issues' in the Late Nineteenth and Twentieth Centuries" (Lewis, 1990).[80] Canadian lesbian mother and academic Katherine Arnup (1990; 1994) also surveyed the role of the Canadian government in educating mothers during the interwar years and examined the advice given to mothers by child care and medical experts in Canada over the 20th century. American scholars Ann Phoenix and Anne Woollett argue in the introduction of their 1991 edited collection *Motherhood: Meanings, Practices and Ideologies* that many groups of mothers are devalued and thus excluded from the two categories of "suitable" and "appropriate" mother because they don't meet the socially constructed ideal of motherhood. The collection critically investigated the representation and treatment of mothers and mothering in psychology, which prescribes and models normative models of mothering in the Western world.

Lesbian and queer parenting became a focus of discussion for feminists during the late 1980s and through the 1990s when identity politics, which was first introduced in the 1970s, developed and took hold in North American feminist thinking, theorizing, teaching, organizing, and research. Understanding that all individuals are shaped by aspects of their identity through gender, race, sexual orientation, class, ability, and religion, lesbians began to speak about their particular experiences as mothers. One of the first articles addressing how lesbian mothering was both a personal and political act was written by Nancy Polikoff and published alongside other groundbreaking chapters in *Politics of the Heart: A Lesbian Parenting Anthology* edited by Sandra Pollack and Jeanne Vaughn in 1987. American sexuality consultant Elena Marie DiLapi added to this rich and developing discussion in her 1989 article "Lesbian Mothers and the Motherhood Hierarchy," when she argued that a motherhood hierarchy privileges and gives priority to different types of mothers, and that through the use of "antilesbian mythology," lesbian women are considered to be "most inappropriate mothers" and are therefore located at the bottom of the motherhood hierarchy.

In 1992, American sociologists Julie Ainslie and Kathryn Feltey published a paper that explored definitions and dynamics of motherhood and family in lesbian communities, while American anthropologist Ellen Lewin wrote a chapter in 1994 that addressed the ways in which lesbian mothers negotiated motherhood through strategies of resistance and accommodation. Katherine Arnup wrote a number of articles and books (1988; 1989; 1995) addressing the realities of lesbian mothering for both mothers and children in Canadian society, while another Canadian sociologist, Fiona Nelson, started to develop "a lesbian maternal discourse" in her 1997 book exploring Canadian lesbian families living in rural Western Canada in the 1990s. In the same year, Kate Griffin and Lisa Molhalland edited a collection of articles entitled *Lesbian Motherhood in Europe*, which addressed lesbian mothering in countries such as Ireland, England, and Norway. American lesbian mother Jess Wells also edited a book that year, *Lesbians Raising Sons,* which addressed the challenges and pleasures lesbians often experience in a society that is hostile to their mothering practices of raising boys to become men.

Other feminist intellectuals continued the work done in the previous decade of critically examining the ideologies of motherhood and attending to the voices of mothers. Developmental psychologist Meryle Mahrer Kaplan (1993), for instance, investigated how a group of upper-middle-class mothers were parenting their toddlers in ways that didn't follow or replicate the traditional image of the self-sacrificing mother. Comparative studies scholar Ann Kaplan (1992) examined the images of mothers in popular culture and melodrama from the 1830s to the 1990s, while American psychologist Shari Thurer traced the development of the ideology of the "good mother" through the shifting ideals and ideologies of motherhood and mothering over the ages in her book *The Myths of Motherhood: How Culture Reinvents the Good Mother*. American Kathryn Keller (1994) also examined the ideology of motherhood and the good mother in popular representations of mothers in women's magazines, specifically from the 1960s to 1980s, and discovered a persistent and continual depiction of the traditional stay-at-home mother, even though more and more mothers were working outside the home than ever before. Advertisements in women's magazines through the 1990s generally depicted employed white middle- and upper-class mothers as caring mothers, while poor and working-class ethnic minority mothers were portrayed primarily as workers.[81]

Contemporary feminism of the 1990s, which was significantly shaped by diversity and difference, appears to have made an uneasy peace with motherhood, although it continued to question how to reconcile successful work with parenting.[82] While there has been discussion about and some movement toward providing better maternal leave for mothers and developing paternal leave programs for fathers, as well as keeping pressure on provincial and federal governments in Canada to provide universal child care for children, these attempts have been met with sporadic mediocre patchwork responses.[83]

As the 20th century drew to a close, British writer of Sierra Leonean and Scottish heritage Aminatta Forna explored the highly idealized concept of Western motherhood in *Mother of All Myths: How Society Moulds and Constrains Mothers* (1999), and demonstrated the ways in which the backlash of the 1980s and 1990s to earlier feminist initiatives and movements for women and mothers reasserts an old-fashioned, conservative, and narrow view of what a mother should be and do through messages in the media, rulings in the courts, legislation of the government, and attitudes and practices in medicine and popular psychology.

Taking a different critical approach to understanding ideology and motherhood, American academics Evelyn Glenn, Grace Chang, and Linda Rennie Forcey brought together an interdisciplinary group of scholars in an edited collection in 1994 who offered "a variety of perspectives on mothering as a socially constructed set of activities and relationships involved in nurturing and caring for people."[84] Two years later, in 1996, American sociologist Sharon Hays published *The Cultural Contradictions of Motherhood* where she introduced the theory and term "intensive mothering" to identify and explain the ideology and standard of mothering that had been socially determined over the past century, and particularly since the 1980s, which assigned mothers across class boundaries and whether "career" or "stay-at-home" moms, the role and status of the ideal and preferred caretaker of their sacred children. To be good mothers, women must feel fulfilled by the endless, labour-intensive, expert-guided, and emotionally absorbing work of raising their children within this intensive model of motherhood.[85]

The voices of marginalized feminists also become more prevalent during the third wave of feminism, in part because of a commitment to diversity by feminists of the time, and in part because publishing and academia had opened up more readily to the experiences and knowledge of folks who have been historically marginalized due to practices such as colonialism, imperialism, and racialization. For instance, multiple writers explored the interconnections among ethnicity, patriarchy, colonialism, racism, and motherhood in two collections published in the early 1990s: *Double Stitch: Black Women Writers Write about Mothers and Daughters* in 1991 and *Food for Our Grandmothers: Writings by Arab-American and Arab-Canadian Feminists* in 1994. Canadian legal and critical race theorist Marlee Kline addressed the law's continued colonialism in child welfare law and policy in her 1993 article "Complicating the Ideology of Motherhood: Child Welfare Law and First Nation Women." American feminist news journal *Off Our Backs* (1970–2008) published a special issue on Feminism and Motherhood in 2006, which featured various articles on the realities of mothering, including raising biracial children and lesbian mothering.

In the 2000s, writings by Indigenous scholars and activists address feminism, mothering and motherhood. Cree/Métis writer Kim Anderson developed a theory of Indigenous ideology of motherhood through her exploration of the role of mothers both historically and currently in Indigenous cultures and the ways in which colonialism, patriarchy, and feminism misunderstand the influence of women's motherwork within these diverse communities in her 2000 and 2007 publications. American English and women's studies scholar Lisa Udel addresses the roles of revision and resistance in the politics of native women's motherwork in a 2001 article, while the 2006 collection *Until Our Hearts Are On the Ground: Aboriginal Mothering, Oppression, Resistance and Rebirth* edited by the mother and daughter duo Jeanette Corbiere Lavell and Dawn Memee Lavell-Harvard speaks of the complex realities of being a mother challenging a patriarchal and racist repressive ideology of motherhood and raises the call for women to reclaim their traditional powers in Aboriginal Canadian cultures.

The end of the century also saw one of the first critiques of contemporary ideologies of breastfeeding (that continues into 2012) in North America with the 1999 publication of Linda

Blum's book *At the Breast: Ideologies of Breast Feeding and Mothering in Contemporary United States*. British author and life coach Jayne Buxton's *Ending the Mother War: Starting the Workplace Revolution* (1998) continued the discussion about working mothers and developed a theory on how the media-created "Superwoman" was pitted against so-called "Earth-mothers" and how this myth muddied debates about working mothers and prevented discussing the real issues associated with mothers successfully combining work and children. Attention to divisions between mothers and the realities of working mothers persisted into the 21st century, with two well received American books, namely, *The Truth Behind the Mommy Wars: Who Decides What Makes a Good Mother?* in 2005, and *Mommy Wars: Stay-at-Home and Career Moms Face Off on Their Choices, Their Lives, Their Families* in 2007. Many magazine articles and commentaries were also published around the so-called Mommy Wars and the divisions among different types of mothers and their child-rearing approaches well into the first decade of the second millennium.[86]

American author and mother Susan Maushart continued the tradition and work begun by feminists in the second wave of speaking honestly about the experiences of mothering and the influence of the socially constructed institution of motherhood in her 2000 book *The Mask of Motherhood: How Becoming a Mother Changes Our Lives and Why We Never Talk About It*. Writer, novelist, journalist, and feminist mother Ariel Gore began the award-winning parenting zine *Hip Mama* in 1993, and followed it up with two books, *The Hip Mama Survival Guide: Advice From the Trenches On: Pregnancy, Childbirth, Cool Names, Clueless Doctors* in 1998 and *The Mother Trip: Hip Mama's Guide to Staying Sane in the Chaos of Motherhood* in 2000, and an edited collection of writings *Breeder: Real-Life Stories from the New Generation of Mothers* in 2001 which, like her zine, focuses on the culture and politics of motherhood. Addressing the realities of mothering for young, poor, single, queer and other marginalized mothers, Gore brought interest and vitality to both maternal feminism and the contemporary mothers' movement. And more recently, Canadian mother and queer activist Rachel Epstein edited a collection of stories in 2010 written by queer parents and their children, as well as queer children in *Who's Your Daddy? And Other Writings on Queer Parenting.*

Well-known American feminist, author, and mother Naomi Wolfe carried on the practice of truth telling in her popular 2001 publication *Misconceptions: Truth, Lies, and the Unexpected on the Journey to Motherhood* where she reflected upon the realities of her own journey into and with motherhood, and provided an analysis, much like Maushart, of the ways in which society and mothers treat women as parents. The same year, Susan Chase and Mary Rogers edited a collection of articles addressing the challenges, joys, and multiple realities and experiences of mothering from the perspectives of a wide range of mothers in *Mothers and Children: Feminist Analysis and Personal Narratives*. Here writers were critical of the institution of motherhood, the ideals of the "good" and "bad" mother, the challenges and benefits of parenting alone, the politics of mothering, and the complexities of conception, childbirth, and parenting. American writer and mother Andrea J. Buchanan candidly examines her own development as a mother in her 2003 book *Mother Shock: Loving Every (Other) Minute of It* and exemplified one of many sub-genre "mommy lit" books and mommy blogs about motherhood, pregnancy and child-rearing that appeared on bookshelves and online in the first decade of the 21st century.[87]

Feminist critics also continued to follow the strategies of the earlier generation when thinking about mothers in North America by addressing the larger social and political picture. For instance, in 2002 American financial writer and author Ann Crittenden published *The Price of Motherhood: Why the Most Important Job in the World is Still the Least Valued* to demonstrate how mothers are systematically disadvantaged and made dependent by a society that exploits those who perform its most crucial work.[88] In 2004, witty American authors Susan Douglas and Meredith Michaels critique thirty years of popular culture, the media's obsession with motherhood, and the impossible standards that obsession promotes in *The Mommy Myth: The Idealization of Motherhood and How It Has Undermined All Women*. And Shari McDonald Strong and Kristin Rowe-Finkbeiner add to the critique of motherhood in 2006 when they edit a collection of thirty articles written by mothers who speak about the challenges of parenting and how they work towards social change in their differing feminisms in *The Maternal Is Political: Women Writers at the Intersection of Motherhood and Social Change*.

Clearly, mothering and motherhood have continued to be of great interest and an area of growth for academic and activist feminists alike at the turn of the 21st century. Perhaps one of the biggest indications and best explanations of its magnitude was the birth in 1998 of the Association for Research on Mothering (ARM) in Toronto, the feminist scholarly and activist organization on mothering and motherhood which, in 2011, was renamed the Motherhood Initiative for Research and Community Involvement (MIRCI). Founded by maternal scholar and feminist mother Andrea O'Reilly, MIRCI is the first international feminist organization devoted specifically to the topic of mothering and motherhood, to actively providing a forum for the discussion and distribution of research on motherhood, and to establishing a community of individuals and institutions working and researching in the area of mothering and motherhood.[89] Within a decade, over 500 scholars, writers, activists, social workers, midwives, nurses, therapists, lawyers, teachers, politicians, parents, students, and artists from more than twenty countries became members.

Understanding the significance of scholarly publications to feminist theorizing and movement, as well as the importance of community building for researchers, academics, activists, and mothers interested in the topic of motherhood, ARM published an academic journal, *Journal of the Association for Research on Mothering*, renamed the *Motherhood Initiative* (JMI) in 2011, addressing the complexities and intersectionality of class, race, sexuality, age, ethnicity, ability, and nationality.[90] Interest, research, and scholarship around the multiple issues concerning mothers, mothering, and motherhood are plentiful. For instance, in its eleven year history from 1999 to 2010, the Journal examined motherhood topics as diverse as: adoption; care work; health; lesbian mothering; literature; mothers and daughters; mothers and sons; mothering, race, and ethnicity; motherhood and feminism; peace; popular culture; public policy; religion and spirituality; sexuality; the motherhood movement; work; young mothers, violence, militarism, war and social justice; and bereavement, loss, and grief.

MIRCI and its Journal, along with Demeter Press, the first peer-reviewed feminist publisher to circulate scholarship on mothering and motherhood within an international context and from a multitude of perspectives, also founded by O'Reilly, have helped to ensure motherhood studies has developed over the past two decades into a vibrant academic field with many international conferences and hundreds of scholarly articles published on a great variety of themes and issues related to mothering and motherhood.[91] Two monumental publications, the anthology *Maternal Theory* (2007) and the three-volume *Encyclopedia on Mothering* (2010), both edited by O'Reilly, and many titles published by Demeter Press underscore the substantial growth and politicalization of maternal scholarship.[92]

The International Motherhood Movement, created in 2008, and the 2011 publication of *The 21st Motherhood Movement*, further demonstrates the expansion of collective organizing around global issues and concerns associated with motherhood. The virtual Museum of Motherhood (MOM), which documents the evolving role of mothers in North America, is indicative of the increasing awareness of and commitment to mothering.[93] Multiple mommy blogs and online communities of mothers including, but not limited to, *Girls Gone Child*, *Latina Mami*, *Literary Mama Mothers Acting Up*, *Mothers & More*, *Mothers Are Women*, *Notes from the Trenches*, and *The Mothers Movement Online* also demonstrate how maternal activism and scholarship are thriving throughout and beyond the first decade of the 21st century.

The Practice of Feminist Mothering

Feminist research and writing on mothering and motherhood continues today with the support of MIRCI's annual international conferences, feminist journal and press, and carries on the tradition of informing feminist scholarship, theorizing, activism, and thinking. However, as seen in the above overview of feminist theorizing on motherhood and mothering, while there has been a consistent challenge to patriarchal motherhood by feminists in feminist organizing, research, activism, and scholarship since the early days of second wave of feminism, "there has been very little academic discourse of the subject of feminist mothering."[94] The complexities of being both a feminist and a mother, which are a reality for many women, have only been minimally investigated within this flourishing field of maternal studies.

One of the first and few feminist scholars to address feminist mothering was American Tuula Gordon with the publication of her edited book *Feminist Mothers* in 1990, where authors honestly address how the facade of patriarchal motherhood hides the realities of motherwork and how many women want to avoid it. Some writers called for a different perspective of motherhood and demonstrate how to implement a theory of motherhood that is free of myths of a blissful state of being. In 1994, American theorists Maureen Reddy, Martha Roth, and Amy Sheldon published a rare collection of writings by non-academic feminist mothers speaking as subjects, rather than as objects of analysis or as daughters of their own mothers in *Mother Journeys: Feminists Write about Mothering* (1994). Other writings during this era tended to focus on the experiences of daughters, or on the relationship between mothers and daughters and the transmission of the values of second wave feminist mothers into the lives of their daughters. Two examples of this approach are American Rose Glickman's 1993 book *Daughters of Feminists* and mother and daughter academic team Christine Looper Baker and Chistina Baker Kline's 1997 book, *The Conversation Begins: Mothers and Daughters talk about Living Feminism*.

Andrea O'Reilly, the prominent and prolific Canadian maternal theorist and scholar has published extensively in the broad area of feminism and motherhood. She has authored two books: *Toni Morrison and Motherhood* (2004), which addresses the influence of Morrison's writing on maternal theory, and *Rocking the Cradle* (2006), which investigates feminism and the possibility of empowered mothering. She has also edited, as of 2011, a dozen books addressing a wide range of significant topics, including the influence of prominent feminists Adrienne Rich and Sara Ruddick on maternal theorizing and practice; the role of feminism in empowered mothering; feminism as it is connected to mothers and daughters, and to mothers and sons; mothering as discourse and practice; mothering, power, and oppression; essential readings in maternal theory; politics, identity, and experience related to motherhood in the 21st century; and the motherhood movement of the 21st century. One of her most recent edited collections, *Feminist Mothering* (2008), "goes beyond critiques of patriarchal motherhood to locate and investigate feminist maternal practices as sites for women's empowerment and social change," particularly the ways in which mothers "integrate activism, paid employment, non-sexist child-rearing practices, and non-child-centered interests in their lives."[95]

American mother, communications professor, and author Amber Kinser published two books, *Mothering in the Third*

Wave and Feminism in 2008 and *Motherhood and Feminism* in 2010, which reflect on the interconnection of feminism and mothering exclusively within the context of the third wave. The collection of articles in *Mothering in the Third Wave* considers how globalization, technology, and popular culture shape the form and content of feminist mothering, while *Motherhood and Feminism* examines the role of feminism within motherhood—specifically what it means to be a good mother, what role mothers play in the family and in society, and how motherhood has been redefined throughout time—and emphasizes the continued need for the expansion of contemporary mother activism that has occurred since the mid 1990s and how the changing world of motherhood fits into third wave feminist activism.[96]

As Kinser notes in the introduction of *Mothering in the Third Wave*, work on mothering in this era is both sparse and predominantly written from the perspective of daughters who are attempting to "move away from traditional family practices and toward more feminist, less prescriptive ones" or are trying to articulate "sources and forms of power that are different from that of the mother's."[97]

An example of this approach can be found in various articles in Daisy Hernandez and Bushra Rehman's 2002 edited collection *Colonize This! Young Women of Color on Today's Feminism*, and in Colleen Mack-Canty and Sue Marie Wright's 2008 article "Parenting in Third Wave Feminism and Empowering All Family Members" in O'Reilly's *Feminist Mothering*. And although publications like the special 2006 Mothers and Feminism double issue of *JARM*, and my monologue *Feminist Mothering in Theory and Practice, 1985–1995: A Study in Transformative Politics,* published in 2009, consider various theories and practices of empowered and feminist mothering, there remains a great need for further thorough exploration and discussion into the lived realities of feminist mothers and how their feminism is translated into the lives of their children.[98]

This need for an ongoing and sustained examination of the lived realities of women mothering as feminists is the motivation for this book, *Practicing Feminist Mothering*, which focuses primarily on how feminist mothers understand, trouble, and consciously dispute the ideology of patriarchal motherhood, how they create parenting based on their own knowledge and experiences of feminist mothering, how they engage in matroreform—the act of claiming motherhood power—and how they construct/create/develop/maintain feminist motherlines—those feminist maternal genealogies that record and ensure that the difficult, yet rewarding feminist motherwork remains a visible communal and political endeavour.

My main objective here is to continue the feminist commitment and work of breaking the silence/s around the realities of mothering and motherhood by investigating the complexities of feminist mothering and to speak honestly about ways in which self-identified feminist mothers defy the master patriarchal discourse of motherhood, while not constructing a feminist master discourse to take its place. While I began this work in the mid 1990s with my PhD research and have published many articles and a book that specifically addresses the ways in which self-identified feminist mothers integrate their feminism with their mothering, and the ways in which their mothering informs their feminism, my aim here, which is similar to what Kinser suggests in her 2008 article examining mothering as a relational consciousness, is to explore the "messiness of feminist mothering," to dislodge the mask of motherhood as theorized by Susan Maushart and its "semblance of serenity and control that enables women's work to pass unnoticed in the larger drama of human life," and to consider the complexities of feminist mothering from the perspectives of mothers.[99]

While mothering is understood within the dominant patriarchal paradigm to be private and apolitical, feminists understand mothering to be political and to have cultural significance.[100] Moving beyond the work of Adrienne Rich, who understands this distinction, and implementing Sara Ruddick's theory and practice of maternal thinking, feminist mothers re/define mothering and their motherwork as a conscious and politically engaged endeavour with the purpose of effecting positive cultural and political change through feminist modes of mothering.[101] As I have demonstrated in my previous research exploring the interconnection and outcome of feminism and mothering, self-identified feminist mothers integrate their feminism and their mothering practices in complex and complicated ways that resist patriarchal motherhood and its expectations of mothering.[102]

Since feminist mothers constantly interrogate the power dynamics of interpersonal relationships (including their own) and larger social systems and structures to understand how gender inequality is produced, maintained, and perpetuated through the ideology and institution of motherhood, they are consistently engaged in the messy, tension-filled, and sometimes conflicting work of uniting their feminism and their parenting. Attempting to be consciously aware means they pay attention to sexist gender relations and child-rearing practices, and remain committed to contesting and converting inequality based on gender binaries, as well as other hierarchies based on culturally constructed categories of people, their beliefs, and their behaviour based on race, sex, gender, ability, class, religion, culture, economics, ideology, and sexuality/sexual orientation.[103]

As in other areas of their lives, feminist mothers take on the challenging work of parenting in ways that bring attention to and dispute these disparities. The purpose of this book is to explore how a particular group of self-identified feminist mothers engage in the complex praxis of feminist mothering where they both theorize and create a practical counternarrative and a functioning living space to engage in alternative ways of parenting that are informed by their feminism.

CHAPTER 2

The Praxis of Feminist Mothering

Investing in the next generation is one of the most political things that you can do, even if it's on a scale as small as your own children.[104]

Like Canadian feminist standpoint theorist Lorraine Code, I understand that knowledge is produced, situated within, and shaped by the specific contexts of time and place, and that specific knowledge/s contribute to various standpoints that are also partial and irrefutably informed by those particular perspectives.[105] By extending the feminist supposition that women have particular lived experiences that assist them in viewing the world in ways that bring about diverse knowledge to also include the experiences of self-identified feminist mothers, I hope to reveal some of the complex ways in which women integrate their feminism into their parenting that enable them to resist the master/dominant discourse of motherhood.

In this chapter, I examine how a small group of self-identified feminist mothers understand feminism, motherhood, and mothering, and how this convergence underpins their conscious practice of feminist parenting. Like Sharon Abby, Amber Kinser, and other feminist scholars, I attempt to understand and explain the maternal experiences of these feminist mothers in a way that honours their particular perspectives without being elitist or exclusionary, and does not romanticize or contribute to the development of a different master discourse within feminist writings on mothering.[106] Rather than prescribe an idealized approach to feminist mothering for others to replicate, I explain one way in which particular self-identified feminist mothers have brought together their feminism and mothering.

I begin by outlining some of the demographic and social markers of the women in this particular group as a way of introducing them and of acknowledging some of their shared similarities and a few of their significant differences. I then offer an overview of how they understand feminism and how their feminist worldview helps them to see and critically question the expectations placed on mothers associated with institutionalized motherhood. I conclude by arguing that mothering is understood by these women to be a political act where they willfully engage in feminist praxis—the conscious act of integrating knowing with doing—by linking their feminism with their mothering to create mothering practices that interrupt the institution of motherhood and offer alternative feminist models of mothering.[107]

Locating Self-Identified Feminist Mothers

In the fall of 1996, as part of my PhD research into the interconnection of feminism and mothering, I had the great fortune to meet and interview sixteen mothers who identified themselves as feminist. During the latter months of 1996 and most of 1997, I met with each woman at least twice to talk about her understandings of feminism, mothering, and the integration of the two in her parenting.

While this group shared the common characteristic of self-identifying as feminist mothers, they also experienced a number of differences. For instance, there was an age range of two decades between the youngest mother, who at the time of the first set of interviews in 1996 was 29, and the eldest who was 50-years-old. At that time, two of the sixteen women were raising non-biological children in addition to biological children. Four mothers were raising children under the age of five years, two had children under the age of thirteen, and six were rearing children between the ages of five and 13. One mother's children were teenaged, while two were mothers of teenage and adult children and one was parenting children between the ages of 10 and adulthood.

Half of the mothers were raising children outside a romantic relationship and the other half were parenting in partnerships. Two mothers identified as lesbian, one as bisexual, eleven as heterosexual, and the sexual orientation of two was unknown. Four identified as poor and the other twelve as middle-class. One woman was born in Guyana, two in the US, two in England, and eleven in Canada. In terms of heritage, one identified as Black Guyanese, one as Métis, and two as Jewish. Two were of Colombian/European ancestry, two were of Jewish/European descent, and eight women were of mixed European heritage. Two were living with physical disabilities, while fourteen were temporarily able-bodied.[108]

In 2005 I again had the opportunity to interview ten members of the original group of sixteen. This time we spoke about their experiences of feminism and mothering over the previous decade and what, if anything, they might do differently should they have the chance to parent their children again.[109] Within those intervening years, five of the ten women had left their intimate relationships, one had birthed another child, one had adopted a baby, and one identified as lesbian rather than as bisexual.

In 2007, I had the chance to meet with five adult daughters of four mothers to talk about how, as daughters of feminist mothers, they understood the influence of their mothers' feminism on their own lives—including their identities, as well as their current or future parenting practices should they later become mothers. I was also fortunate to interview a mother/daughter pair about the ongoing influences of feminist mothering in their lives; the daughter was the mother of two pre-teenaged children, making her own mother a grandmother. While the two women had always been close, this mother/daughter duo were particularly connected at this time because the mother of the pair had just adopted an infant daughter, placing her in the distinctive position of again being a mother raising a young child, and locating her daughter in the unique situation of being a sister to a sibling younger than her own children, and whose advice was being sought by her own mother because she was more familiar with the current expectations of parenting a young child.

Even though the personal histories and locations of this group of mothers vary, all were female-identified biological women living in or close to Winnipeg, Manitoba, during the 1990s and the first decade of the 2000s, a time period encompassing a transition from the latter part of the second wave to the beginning of third wave of feminism in North America. All women had some post-secondary education and understood, like African-American feminist bell hooks that "feminists are made, not born."[110] While there isn't space here to delve into each of their stories, nor into the rich understanding each has of feminism, I draw upon excerpts from some of our interviews over the span of a dozen years to flesh out some of their common understandings of feminism below.[111]

Understanding Feminism

During our conversations, each of the sixteen feminist mothers I interviewed willingly identified as feminist and shared distinct memories of their feminist awakenings and development of their feminist consciousness. By drawing upon those discussion, I have been able to identify five distinct characteristics that define what feminist means to them. Feminism is an embodied identity and worldview that entails acknowledging and critiquing patriarchy, understanding how the personal is political, recognizing and demanding autonomy and choice for all (and particularly for women), and putting one's feminist understanding and theorizing into everyday practice.

This section of the chapter is divided into these five distinct, yet interrelated, elements of feminism and features a number of the women's voices to exemplify each characteristic. Each characteristic builds upon the previous, and by the end of the discussion a clear picture of what feminism means to these women is evident.

An Embodied Worldview

While the timing of coming to a feminist consciousness and feminist identity varied for each woman, with some identifying as feminist during adolescence and others as young adults—often when they attended middle or high school, university, or other post-secondary education institutions, or participated in the labour force—by the time of our interviews, they all noted that being feminist was central to their sense of themselves and to the way they understood the world around them and their place within it.

Simply put, being feminist is integral to each woman's sense of self and to her life. Rather than being a role, theory, or ideological paradigm that they take on, being feminist is an embodied experience and worldview that permeates their thinking, beliefs, and actions. All of the women speak of feminism being vital to who they are.

In the spring of 2007, I met with Shar to talk about her experiences of feminist mothering. Although we had met only a few times over the past dozen years or so, we fell easily into conversation and caught up on what had happened since we had met two years before. Being the eldest feminist mother of the group, Shar was almost 62-years-old in 2007. Two of her four children, her 36-year-old biological son and her 34-year-old adopted daughter, were doing well and living in Montreal. Her eldest biological daughter, aged 39 years and living in Winnipeg, was also doing well, having recently divorced her husband and the father of her two pre-teenaged children. Shar's youngest child was her four-year-old daughter, who she had adopted two years previously.

Shar described herself as a single, heterosexual Euro-Canadian feminist woman, who sees feminism as being essential to her being. She explained:

> Feminism is my foundation at this point. It's the basic mud that I move out into the world from. There isn't anything that isn't affected by that. It affects all my relationships, it affects how I think about things, affects how I read a book, affects how I rage against the TV news, just absolutely everything. It's not just a theory; it doesn't feel like it's separate from me.

Jody, too, expressed the fundamental nature of feminism to her identity more than once in our interviews. When we met in early 2005, Jody had recently separated from her husband and father of their 14-year-old son and 12-year-old daughter. She was also dealing with chronic and debilitating knee pain as she anticipated her 44th birthday the following month and the timing of knee joint replacement surgery. When I asked her what feminism meant to her, she replied, "It's a way of thinking, an understanding of self and of where women fit within the scheme of life and the world." She continued, "You know, when it's ingrained in you, you just ARE it and you don't need a definition for it. It's just who you are and the philosophies that you embrace."

The embodied sense of being a feminist described here by Shar and Jody is shared by all mothers. Further examples of this perspective and experience are illustrated by other feminist mothers throughout the chapter in excerpts from interviews illustrating the other elements of their feminist mothering to which I now turn.

Acknowledging and Critiquing Patriarchy

When I asked Jody to elaborate on the philosophy that she embraced as a feminist, she told me understanding and critiquing patriarchy was a core element of her feminism. Again, Jody was not alone in this understanding. The other feminist mothers articulated that they, too, recognized that we live in a patriarchal society, a society based upon an unjust social system that creates and supports the role of the male as the primary authority figure, which is central to and is supported by familial, legal, political, economic and social organization. Their feminism demands a critique of patriarchy that is understood to be oppressive to all, as it limits everyone to varying degrees according to, but not limited to, one's sex, gender, class, race/ethnicity, sexual orientation, ability, and age. More specifically, patriarchy efficiently disempowers and disenfranchises children and women through systemic discrimination that supports and maintains a male-dominated hierarchy. Fundamental to understanding and questioning patriarchy is the act of intentionally asking and analyzing what, where, when, why, and how patriarchy operates in the everyday, and exploring its implications in people's lives. Three feminist mothers, Andrea, Laura, and Tammy illustrate the significance of this approach below.

In the fall of 1997, I met with Andrea, a 44-year-old, middle-class, able-bodied Euro-Canadian. Andrea had recently stopped working and pursuing an M.A. in Women's Studies to move, with her husband, from Ontario back to Winnipeg to be closer to her family of origin. As we visited in her home, where she was spending most of her time raising her one-and-a-half-year-old daughter while her husband worked in his office upstairs as a self-employed designer, Andrea explained her understanding of patriarchy in this way:

> I think the world is run primarily by men, and primarily by White men, and that there's a power structure that we all fit into. It's important if we're White, for instance, to recognize that there's privilege that comes along with a skin colour. Or, if we're male, we should be recognizing that there's privilege that comes with that. It's not so much that we all have our own little place, but that there are different power structures, and to see who has the power in our country, or in our world, or in our community.

Laura, aged 38 years, was also an able-bodied stay-at-home mother during the time of our interviews. We met twice over an eight-month period between the fall of 1996 and the spring of 1997 when Laura was on maternity leave from a local university where she was teaching. During our second visit, while Laura's husband played with their older two-year-old in the warm weather in the neighbourhood park, Laura nursed her recently birthed infant daughter and described how patriarchy was central to her feminism:

> Being a feminist is recognizing that there are systemic structures in society that limit everyone and support everyone in different degrees, and systematically limit women in certain ways which are harmful. I think they limit men as well, but they limit and support them in ways that give them power. They limit women in ways that allow them to be systematically disempowered and disenfranchised and I believe that's wrong and I take whatever steps I can to fight it. That's what being a feminist is.

During our third interview in 2005, Tammy, an able-bodied, 46-year-old, middle-class Euro-Canadian living with her common-law male partner and their 18-year-old daughter and their 15- and seven-year-old sons, described how she understood, in her words, "the machine of patriarchy." Her account expands upon the explanation of patriarchy given by Andrea and Laura to include the role of the economic structure:

> The stereotype, in many ways, is based on the wealthy White man. However, it goes beyond that. I think it's more insidious. It's in the whole economic structure. It's not only what used to be just multinational corporations. It's coalitions of financial agencies with their intricate relationships with each other, and governments that do things that keep them alive or that allow for more and more profit making. And people who make those decisions are primarily rich White men, but there are some rich White women, and there are some rich Asian men and rich Black men, although probably less likely than rich White men.

> So it's got more to do with the machine of patriarchy itself than with any of the people who are fighting for it. It's the culture itself, the whole consumerist, conventional, individualistic, very superficial, caring about very small concerns as opposed to having a broader view and caring about the people who are next to them.

The Personal is Political

Being feminist for these women entails more than identifying, understanding, and critiquing patriarchy. It also includes an understanding that what people do as individuals has an influence on the larger world and that what occurs in the larger world has an effect on each individual. In other words, being feminist includes an understanding that the personal and political are thoroughly entwined because all humans have varying degrees of agency and influence in the world and all people are variously influenced by the world around them.

The following explanation given by Tammy clearly demonstrates her understanding of the interconnection of the personal and political, particularly in how the work of raising children contributes to society as a whole. She notes being aware of her position as a mother and the influence she has on her children, who, in turn, have an impact upon the world, just as the world affects all of them:

> When I was really young, before I had any children—when I thought, "Do I want any children or not?"—I saw having children as making a contribution to society in that you're going to school them in a culture and an orientation. They were going to be people who were maybe different or the same, but they were going to have an impact. It wasn't neutral. It's the next society, the next generation, and how you raise them is going to have a huge difference on what our future's like. For sure it's political.
>
> It's a consciousness of being part of a larger society and of your actions having an effect on a larger society. So taking

> responsibility for that and saying, "Well, it's political because it just radiates well beyond where we are here and now."

Shar, the able-bodied single 62-year-old mother of four and grandmother of two pre-teens quoted at the beginning of this section on understanding feminism also has a clear understanding of the interconnection between the personal and the political, which she shared with me late one afternoon after all of the children had been picked up from her home-based child care. She told me:

> Everything is political. There is no such thing as separating things out and saying, "This is political and this is not, or this is social and this is economic, or this is family and this is community." There's no such thing. Everything we do in society has political implications. Everything we do in interacting with anybody else is political.

Kim, a Jewish 36-year-old, heterosexual, able-bodied mother who was living with the father of their two sons, aged six and two years, when we first met to talk about feminist mothering, provides a good summary of how these women generally understand feminism. In an interview that took place in a classroom at a local university on a cool fall weekend in 1996, Kim shared how the intersection of the personal and political is a keystone of her feminism and how being feminist is seamlessly integral to her sense of self and her life:

> Feminism is something I almost don't think about anymore because it's so integrated with who I am that I don't think about it. So what does it mean to me? Making the personal political has always been the basic foundation for my feminism. Looking at how you are in your day-to-day life, and how that connects up with the big picture in terms of where women fit. I try to broaden my definition of feminism to include other "isms." So often feminism gets relegated to "Oh, you're just worried about women. And obviously I am concerned about women, but I try to include homophobia, racism, and sexism into my definition of feminism. So it's

> connecting the personal with the political, seeing the connections between all the different "isms."

Autonomy and Choice

All of these feminists believe that autonomy and choice are central to human self-determination and to freeing folks from the social construction of gender and its resulting limitations. The fundamental right for all people to make personal decisions about themselves and their lives is closely connected to understanding how patriarchy operates and to the interrelationship between the personal and the political. Ensuring that women can make choices in their lives regarding—among others—relationships, education, work, religion, reproduction, family, children, and mothering is another key component of their feminism. Engaging in conscious decisions, and making choices whenever possible, is one way they personally take charge of their lives and create social change.

Andrea, the stay-at-home 44-year-old mother of a one-and-a-half-year-old daughter, introduced earlier in the discussion on understanding and critiquing patriarchy, explains her understanding and the importance of choice to her:

> In its simplest form, choice is about believing in and actively working toward equality in all aspects. It's important for us as women to have choices, to know that we have choices, and to understand what they are, and that we have the ability to make them. It obviously can go deeper than that, but that's the easiest short answer.

Jody, the 46-year-old mother of an adolescent son and daughter, who also addressed patriarchy earlier, elaborates on the meaning of choice when she speaks about what being feminist means to her:

> To me it means the opportunity or the right to choose what's best for me, of knowing what's best for me and not being pushed from other people's standpoints; to know that I know myself enough to make the right decisions for myself, and to be able to have that choice.

Praxis

Clearly, feminism for these mothers extends beyond a mere theoretical understanding of patriarchy, the personal being political, and autonomous choice. It also encompasses the conscious act of putting those theoretical and experiential understandings of feminism into action. In other words, feminism for these mothers means engaging in praxis, the practice of integrating knowing with doing. For example, Paula, a 40-year-old, chemically sensitive, separated, heterosexual, working-class mother of two daughters, aged 11 and four years, and an eight-year-old son, shared how she personally engaged in praxis during an interview in 1997: "Feminist, to me, is political and it inspires action; both outward kinds of actions, like attending demonstrations and the way I raise my children, and more inward sorts of actions, like how I run my life." One specific example of how feminism is political for Paula is her decision to live in a feminist and woman-only cooperative that supports her choices and feminist worldview and where her philosophy and practical decisions about her life and the life of her children are understood and supported. The relevance and significance of Paula's choice to live in the women's co-op are discussed more fully in Chapter Four.

Beverly, a single, middle-class, able-bodied mother of two daughters, also spoke of the importance of feminist praxis in her life. In 1997, at age 44, Beverly identified as bisexual and was an activist working for social change, primarily around issues of sexuality and poverty. She lived with her 17-year-old high school daughter, while her 20-year-old daughter lived and attended university in Toronto. Beverly particularly noted the relevance of feminism in her paid work during the late 1990s, when she was educating folks about homophobia and sexism in the helping professions:

> You can't talk about feminism and the patriarchy and equality without bringing in all of the other people who are oppressed and making those linkages. We talk about sexism. We talk about racism. We talk about ageism and ableism.

> We're talking about the same things here. We're talking about a society that does not value diversity. I believe more and more strongly that it's really important for us to make the links, 'cause if we don't make the links, then we're working in isolation.
>
> I think feminism is about a collective process, and asking where the power in this society is, and who's got the privileges. The more we can work together as oppressed groups, the more we've got a fighting chance at making some inroads. But as long as we stay in our separate little communities and do our little work, that's exactly what the power brokers want us to be doing. So it's more and more important that we work together, especially as things get tighter and tighter and the right gets stronger.

Being feminist for these women includes, but is not limited to, seeing, analyzing and understanding patriarchy and the resulting system of social inequality—particularly inequalities pertaining to women and children—that is based on various intersecting forms of privilege and oppression. Their feminism also entails knowing that putting one's personal understandings, beliefs, theories, and knowledge into practice individually and collectively and acts upon their potential and capacity to be self-determined, self-directed, and engaged social-change agents in the world.

A good example of this understanding of feminism is explained by Lynette, a 29-year-old, able-bodied, middle-class, heterosexual, married mother I spoke with in 1997, when she was dividing her time between raising her one- and three-year-old sons at home, and working part-time at an agency dedicated to senior aged women. Lynette reflected on some of the paid work she was doing around empowerment with older women as she explained her understanding of the dynamics of power and the importance of encouraging political changes through personal awareness and action:

> I see myself as having the right to the same power and status as anybody else in society, and that other women, whether they are older or younger, also have the same rights and

> power as other people in society. I try and do something about that in terms of personal empowerment in the training that I do with older women.

Lynette and the other feminist mothers I interviewed recognize that what they do, whether individually or collectively, affects personal lives and the larger world. Their understanding and practice meets the characterization of feminism noted by Canadian feminist and motherhood scholar Sharon Abby:

> Briefly stated, feminism can be defined by any number of descriptors such as: a very personal act; a struggle against sexism, racism and classism as paradigms for all oppression; a woman's assertion of her own power and a refusal to compromise; a commitment to end white male domination; the creation of inclusivity and mutuality; and the insistence on the well-being of all women.[112]

The collective understanding and practice of feminism by these particular mothers also acknowledges the demand for equality and freedom of individual choice, recognizes that women are autonomous beings, critiques the intersectionality of various "isms" and phobias (such as homophobia and transphobia), and is committed to contesting the structures of hierarchy and patriarchy, as many third wave feminists do.[113]

Having articulated the meaning of feminism to these particular mothers, I next explore how their feminism informs their understanding of motherhood. However, before doing so, I first address the institution of motherhood as understood by various feminist theorists who engage in maternal theory.

The Institution of Motherhood

> Perhaps by revealing the traps, and tracing how we have arrived at current ways of thinking about motherhood, we can blow the most destructive of these myths away all together and move to a new approach to raising children...one in which the model of motherhood embraces woman in all her

> roles instead of placing her needs and other interests in conflict with the function of parenting.[114]

Motherhood scholars recognize the distinction between two tightly overlapping and defining elements of motherhood originally identified by American, lesbian, feminist theorist, poet and mother Adrienne Rich in *Of Woman Born* published in 1976. The first encapsulates "the *potential* relationship of any woman to her powers of reproduction and to children," while the second refers to "the *institution*—which aims at ensuring that that (sic) potential—and all women—shall remain under male control."[115] Motherhood, in other words, entails mothering—the interpersonal relations and work involved in raising children that is generally taken up by women—and the prescribed ideals of mothering, which are often experienced as oppressive because of the narrowly constituted and institutionalized patriarchal rules and expectations that dictate familial and child rearing roles, responsibilities and relationships among women, children, and men.

Central to understanding women's experiences of mothering is recognizing that motherhood is not restricted to merely bearing and/or caring for children—which themselves take enormous amounts of energy and commitment—but that motherhood also includes the culmination of social structures and meanings that create conditions under which women are expected to parent and, thus, prescribe and shape the circumstances of women's lives. Simply put, women are not at liberty to mother in ways they may consider suitable or appropriate for themselves and their children. Rather, they are pressured to parent within socially prescribed and supported ideals and conditions that are often restrictive and damaging.

Rich argues that while the apparent invisible institution of motherhood is made up of a number of connecting fibres that cannot be touched or seen because there is "no symbolic architecture," nor "visible embodiment of authority, power, or...actual violence," patriarchal motherhood is nevertheless real. Its tangible and harmful effects do in fact "determine our relationship to our children, whether we like to think so or not" and are often felt by women in the following ways:[116]

> Marriage as economic dependence, as the guarantee to the man of "his" children; the theft of childbirth from women; the concept of the "illegitimacy" of a child born out of wedlock; the laws regulating contraception and abortion; the cavalier marketing of dangerous birth control devices; the denial that work done by women at home is part of "production"; the chaining of women in links of love and guilt; the absence of social benefits for mothers; the inadequacy of child-care facilities in most parts of the world; the unequal pay women receive as wage-earners, forcing them often into dependence on a man; the solitary confinement of "full-time motherhood"; the token nature of fatherhood, which gives a man rights and privileges over children toward whom he assumes minimal responsibility; the psychoanalytic castigation of the mother; the pediatric assumption that the mother is inadequate and ignorant; [and] the burden of emotional work borne by women in the family.[117]

Constituted through the development of other institutions—such as the gendered economy, religion, business, medicine, education, law, and the media—motherhood is a dominant patriarchal institution. The family, and the socialization of children within the family, also contributes to sustaining the social production and practice of institutionalized motherhood that demands a particular kind of mothering role be played by women, which is described by Rich in this way: "Institutionalized motherhood demands of women maternal 'instinct' rather than intelligence, selflessness rather than self-realization, relation to others rather than the creation of self. Motherhood is 'sacred' so long as its offspring are 'legitimate'—that is, as long as the child bears the name of a father who legally controls the mother."[118]

Canadian feminist, psychologist, and maternal mental health scholar Gina Wong-Wylie argues that girls and women bear the sociocultural pressures that are informed by cultural narratives that convey shared ideas about what it means to be female which, in turn, play out in culturally entrenched gendered identities and activities such as mothering.[119] Through their socialization, girls and women are exposed to and internalize social and cultural messages about what it means to be a good woman and a good mother, given that the two are strongly interconnected.[120]

According to American feminist theorist Suzanne Pharr, for the process of internalized oppression to transpire, people must live within an environment where there is a norm or a standard of rightness by which they are judged. Because negative images and stereotypes of people who do not comply with the norm or the ideal are "backed up by violence, victim-hating and blaming, all of which leads to low self-esteem and self-blame," individuals come to accept the norm and to adopt negative messages and stereotypes of others and of themselves for non-compliance to the ideal.[121] People experience internalized oppression when they believe that their own oppression and the oppression of others is "deserved and should not be resisted."[122]

Within North American society, the good woman/mother standard is presented and normalized through the unsolicited remarks, advice, and/or personal judgments made by physicians, child-rearing experts, teachers, friends, family, and strangers. The good mother is narrowly described as a heterosexual woman who is married to the father of their biological children, is committed to her children's well-being and is not active in the labour force. Building upon the theory of intensive mothering defined and explained by Sharon Hays in *The Cultural Contradictions of Motherhood*, Canadian feminist, mother, and maternal scholar Andrea O'Reilly outlines eight interrelated elements that make up what she terms "sacrificial motherhood" so essential to the current dominant discourse in North America:[123]

1. Children can only be properly cared for by their biological mother.
2. This mothering must be provided 24/7.
3. The mother must always put her children's needs before her own.
4. Mothers must turn to the experts for instruction.
5. The mother is fully satisfied, fulfilled, completed, and composed in motherhood.
6. Mothers must lavish excessive amounts of time, energy, and money in the rearing of their children.
7. The mother has full responsibility, but no power from which to mother.
8. Motherwork, and child rearing more specifically, are regarded as personal, private undertakings with no political import.

According to Hays, O'Reilly, and Susan E. Chase and Mary Rogers, the authors of *Mothers and Children: Feminist Analysis and Personal Narratives*, the "good mother" loves her children unconditionally, puts her children's needs before her own, stays at home to raise her children, and depends upon her spouse to provide for the family. If she is employed and therefore unable to stay at home, she arranges her work schedule around that of her children so she can be with them as much as possible.[124] She educates herself about child development and closely follows the advice of medical and child rearing "experts" she sees on TV and the Internet, hears on podcasts and radio/TV talk shows, or reads online, in newspapers, magazines, and specialty books. From these experts she learns how to identify the standards of the exemplary, as well as the incompetent mother, and how to make sure she becomes the best possible parent she can be. A good mother's success is reflected in her children's polite and respectful behaviour.[125] Should she forget, she is quickly reminded of the legitimacy of the ideal mother and the righteous downfall of the "bad mother" by other mothers, social workers, law and justice officials, educators, medical professionals, and faith/religious leaders.[126] Her peers, co-workers, acquaintances, and other people also perpetuate the dominant expectations of motherhood through their generous attention and unsolicited advice.

Yet, most folks know that this ideal is far removed from the reality of many women's lives. For example, more mothers are working in the labour force in Canada than ever before. In 2004, 65% of all women with children under the age of three, and 70% of women whose youngest child was aged three to five years, worked for pay.[127] Statistics Canada indicates that in 2006, 18% of all children under the age of 15 years lived with a lone parent, and single women, who have historically been among the most economically disadvantaged families in the country, made up 80% of lone parents in Canada.[128] While data about the sexuality of mothers are unavailable, being lesbian or queer does not exclude women from being mothers.[129] Some lesbian and queer mothers have had heterosexual relations with men; others have used alternative or artificial insemination methods to become pregnant, while others have adopted or fostered children. Clearly, not all mothers are married, not all mothers are heterosexual, and the majority of mothers do not stay out of the work force to solely raise children at home.

While the institution of motherhood is pervasive, it is not entirely ironclad. Different women experience motherhood and mothering in various ways depending upon their cultural heritage and practices, socio-economic class, education, religious or philosophical beliefs, ability, gender identity, and/or sexual orientation. Some mothers may be more aware than others of the imposed restrictions, and more or less vulnerable—according to their social class, ethnicity, mental ability and physical capacity—to the various punishments inflicted upon them for not staying within the bounds of the prescribed ideal of motherhood.

The Patriarchal Structure of Family and Motherhood

> The whole construct of motherhood really gets under my skin.[130]

The feminist mothers I spoke with understand the distinction made by Rich that motherhood is both a socially constructed restrictive patriarchal institution and a potentially empowering personal experience. Like Jody, quoted above, they are critical of conventional motherhood, which they understand to be constructed and maintained by various social forces. They are aware of the social pressures placed upon women to conform to socially defined and monitored constructions of the ideal/perfect/good mother that is fundamental to the institution of motherhood.

Below I draw on interviews with four women, namely Neire, Beverly, Jody, and Laura, who represent the group as a whole, to reveal how they are aware of this distinction and are critical of the regulation and harm inflicted on women and children by the institution of motherhood. They expose the power and damaging aspects of its regulations, and specifically notice the ways in which the construct of motherhood is patriarchal in form and endorses the virtues of the stereotypical "good mother" and promotes forewarnings about the dangers of the "bad mother." They acknowledge, and are critical of, the consequences inflicted on mothers and the negative repercussions imposed on children and men resulting from the patriarchal conventional expectations of motherhood that systematically devalue and oppress women. Their perspectives are informed by their feminism, and more specifically, by their critical understanding of patriarchy, their belief that the personal is political, their respect for autonomy and choice, and their commitment to enacting feminist praxis in their daily lives.

When Neire, a 41-year-old, Jewish, Euro-Canadian mother, and I met in 1997, she was adjusting to her recent divorce from her husband and the father of their teenage daughter and their 10- and six-year-old sons. Her identity was evolving in other ways as well; she had recently begun to identify as lesbian and was negotiating a long-distance same-sex relationship.[131] As a full-time nurse and student pursing a BA, Neire was extremely busy, yet she was able to make time to meet with me four times over ten months to talk about feminist mothering. The following is an excerpt from one of our conversations when Neire spoke candidly about her perception of the patriarchal social expectations placed on mothers within the institution of motherhood and its associated damages for women and children:

> I think that society still sees mothers as being women who totally devote themselves to their kids. If the kid has a problem, as a mother you are completely tuned into that kid. And I mean, any variation on that is still seen as not being acceptable. In other words, the mother is still very much responsible for her kids and their actions and their behaviours and their whole being. And when your kid does something wrong, the mother is still blamed. That's still very prevalent.
>
> I think it boils down to this whole ideology surrounding the family, that the family has two people, opposite sexes, and the children. And they're fully enclosed, a supposedly fully functioning family unit. And our society is still predicated on that. So if a woman finds herself in a position where she's not within that structure, the society only pays lip service to supports and that kind of thing.
>
> I think it's very harmful because it doesn't give women, as I say, a sense of their own abilities, a sense of their own power. It puts women down. Like I was saying on Tuesday, if you do something that doesn't fit with a societal concept of what a "good mother" is, you're automatically labelled a "bad mother." And I think there is still this incredible sense of guilt among mothers. We don't talk about it anymore because it's under the surface like a lot of things are in society.
>
> But I think, given that this patriarchal model is still very much in existence, there are still a lot of women who are

> falling into this trap, and it just creates a hell of a lot of conflict and a hell of a lot of guilt. I think it's very damaging. It's definitely damaging to mothers because it erodes our self-esteem and our self-confidence in our ability to be good mothers.

Neire is critical of the patriarchal model of the family and believes that women who try to meet its expectations are likely to fall into its "trap" where women have little or no support when they don't conform to its ideal standards of motherhood. Like Rich, and other feminists, she understands that labelling mothers as "good" and "bad," and the use of violence and threats of violence, are used to control women's mothering practices.[132] She also understands, as do sociologists and other feminists, that children are often removed from lesbian/queer mothers, racialized mothers, and economically impoverished mothers when they are judged to be "bad."[133]

Neire believes the unrealistic and inappropriate ideals imposed on mothers through the institution of motherhood erode women's self-esteem and self-confidence in their ability to parent, and that women lose their ability to be self-directed mothers when they attempt to conform to the patriarchal models of family and motherhood. Like American maternal theorist Sara Ruddick, who argues that women are policed by "the gaze of others," Neire proposes that women feel conflict and guilt for not parenting according to the patriarchal standard rather than feel empowered by their own parenting abilities.[134]

Being critical of the patriarchal structures of family and motherhood and their negative ramifications, particularly of the damage mothers suffer, is important to other feminist mothers. For instance, Beverly—the mother of two daughters aged 17 and 20 years who was introduced earlier in the discussion regarding feminist praxis—believes "the whole system is out of whack" and specifically identifies how the best interests of mothers and children are not promoted within it. Similar to the other feminist mothers, Beverly draws upon her feminist understanding of the power dynamics of patriarchy, reflected upon her own experiences of mothering, and observes and talks with other mothers about their parenting to come to her understanding and critique of motherhood.

During a conversation late one winter afternoon during the tail end of a snowstorm, Beverly explained how the move away from the extended family to the nuclear family in the West and the resulting myths associated with mothering contribute to the restrictions and damage mothers experience:

> It's just so prevalent in our society, that we seem to think that women have this biological, intrinsic nature that we're supposed to know how to mother. And perhaps therein lays the problem. Because I don't think we do. I mean, you just have to look at the mother of a first-born; why are our second-born children so much more at ease with themselves than our first-born children? Because our first-born children were being held in arms that weren't entirely sure that they were holding the baby the right way, or that they were feeding them the right way or all those different things.
>
> There's this huge myth that I think we've all bought into, that we can do this alone, with no help. And then there's the myth that your husband's going to help you, and he doesn't know how to. Another myth is that you're going to turn to your mother at times when you're stressed, and she's going to tell you what to do. When you know damn well that the only thing that she's going to tell you to do is what she did to you, which you don't want to repeat.

Just as the other feminist mothers, Beverly believes the nuclear family structure continues to be the idealized standard family type within the institution of motherhood and the one that people are expected to re/produce and live. She posits that many mothers today experience isolation because of the emphasis on this family type and the loss of the extended family.

Having been both a mother in a nuclear family with two young children and a single parent of a teenaged and an adult daughter, Beverly has experienced the isolating realities of mothering in both models. She is particularly critical of the isolation and low self-esteem that many mothers endure, especially when they lack substantial support within and beyond the family due to the myth that women have a natural ability to easily mother. Just like Neire and feminist maternal scholars, Beverly criticizes motherhood for restricting and trapping mothers with its unrealistic and destructive conditions, and for damaging women's self-esteem by demanding that they devote their lives to, and be solely responsible for, raising their children in the isolating conditions of society.

Understanding the Script of the "Good Mother/Bad Mother"

Similar to feminist theorizing and to the experiences of other mothers in this group, Jody—the mother of two teenage children—is both aware of and critical of the "good mother/bad mother" dichotomy within motherhood discourse. During one of our earlier interviews, Jody describes the "perfect" mother and addresses the pervasiveness of this idealized and mythical image within the media:

> What is the perfect mother? And the concept that society puts on the word "mother"? She's totally responsible for caring, for nurturing, always has a connection with the baby; never have an ill feeling against your child. You would never do anything to harm that child or have harmful thoughts. And I think you get caught up in what you're supposed to be, you know? I think in some ways it's just kinda placed on you.
>
> "The Mother" is in every image, everything you read, everything you see in media, TV; "This is a happy, joyful moment. This will be easy for you. Wow, it will be wonderful." All that kind of stuff and not the reality of what it really is. So when it's not reality, especially the whole thing about, "You should never strike your child, you should never harm your child," you are really frustrated and you suddenly do something. And all you can do is feel guilty. Your child wasn't hurt. But you had that real strong thought, like you might, you could, "throw this baby through the window at any point." And you're not supposed to have those thoughts

> or feelings. Or people say to you, "Oh, you couldn't do anything like that." Guess what? [Laughter] Wrong!
>
> It's been internalized in us. From the time you're little. I mean, in the media. Everything is just the mother whose got the perfect dress on and the perfect kids. The kids are always happy, there's never anything wrong with her kids. And if something happens with the kids, it always comes back to the mother. It's her fault. Well, not necessarily [laughter]. These are individual people making choices too. At what point can we stop blaming the mother? And I think we all get caught up in that, it's a daily struggle.
>
> As for me, I find as a mother, I look at myself and think, "I thought I'd never do that, I thought I'd never say that!" Because it's been ingrained that is what a mother is in some wonderful, sweet poem that you read [laughter] *Mommie Dearest*. Like, there's just never something in between. It's either you're this god-like figure or you're the devil. And it's got to be challenged, constantly.

Jody's account reveals her awareness of the insidiousness of the ideal mother and the role the media plays in promoting it. She is critical of the pressure women endure to internalize expectations of the "perfect" mother and how she personally continues to struggle with these internalized messages and beliefs. Like the other feminist mothers and feminist scholars, she recognizes how the media projects negative images, stereotypes and messages about mothers and promotes practices that coerce mothers to conform to this narrow and unrealistic standard of mothering.[135] Women often internalize the standard by which they are measured to be "good mothers," develop low self-esteem, and blame themselves when they do not meet the criteria associated with this ideal. Having internalized the standard of the "good mother" they believe themselves to be "bad mothers" for non-compliance to the stereotypical mother. Through using tactics such as mother-blaming and labelling women as "bad" in the media, women may feel trapped, as Jody has, between the "god-like figure" and "the devil."

Seeing and Articulating the Limitations of Motherhood

My interview with Laura in 1997 also demonstrates how these feminist mothers understand the discourse of the "good mother" as well as the limitations and dangers of the power imbalance often experienced within the patriarchal family structure. Laura, a 38-year-old, middle-class, Jewish mother on maternity leave with her newborn and two-year-old daughters, easily describes the perfect mother idealized within the institution as a middle-class, married woman who takes on the qualities associated with the "stereotypical" wife, including being apolitical because non-family activities are believed to draw women away from their primary child-rearing and familial responsibilities. As she describes the characteristics expected of the ideal/good mother, Laura illustrates how treating the needs and wants of other family members as much more important than those of the mother's creates and enforces power relationships within the family that are skewed to favour men and disadvantage women and children. She also reasons that male partners, husbands, and fathers have the ability to suppress the needs and desires of other family members as long as they hold the economic power and decision-making authority proscribed in this model:

> Oh, mothers are, according to the image, nurturing, and they stay home if they're good mothers. Of course, then we can nail them for not making money and being welfare moms, unless they have rich husbands. It's okay to stay home if you have a rich husband. They never get mad. They have lots of time to do everything. They keep a pristine home. They make homemade meals and lots of home-baked cookies and breads. They take the kids on outings. It's combined with the stereotype of housewife and that's one of the problems. So they have dinner on the table for their husbands when they come home at 5:30. They sometimes nag their children, but they're supposed to. It's a kind of a good thing-bad thing. They clean up after everybody. They do all of the house cleaning.

> They're sweet. They're volunteers. They go out and drive children around wherever all the children need to be driven. They sit on the PTA [Parent Teacher Association]. They're active only in family things. They're not politically active. They don't go to *Take Back the Night* marches, but they'll be involved in things that affect their children. And the stereotype of mother is they'd rather have the [books] removed from the library, not that they'd stand up for freedom of access to books of which they disapproved. When those issues come up, they want to protect their children and that is their number one goal in life and in everything.
>
> And their only goal, actually, is to protect and take care of and keep a nice, happy, safe home. They don't curse. They don't have sex. How they have kids, I don't know, 'cause they don't have sex. They don't do anything for themselves. Everything they do is for their kids and husbands.

As she further examines the stereotypical perfect mother, Laura articulates several damaging features of motherhood for women, children, and men:

> Real people should take care of themselves. Nobody should value themselves so little that they come behind everybody, including their kids, including their spouse. Real people shouldn't limit their options in the world so profoundly. Yes, you limit your options to some extent. That's just practical, but not so thoroughly as the stereotype. It's harmful for them, and it's harmful for the kids, whether they're boys or girls. It teaches girls to be stunted human beings, if you actually live that way. And it teaches boys to expect stunted human beings, and expect a slave.
>
> And, you know, there are aspects of the stereotype that are wonderful. Those are the parts, obviously, that I think I try to live, the nurturing, the caring, and that stuff. But the self-abnegation is awful, and the not being out in the world, to me, is not being a full person. And I don't mean necessarily working for money. I just mean being a presence in the world, being active and doing things. And you can't do that when your life is one hundred percent involved around your

> home. And, it's bad for the woman. It's bad for the husband! I don't think having a slave is good for people. I think power corrupts and the more you feel that you have somebody at your beck and call, the more corrupting it is. So, I think it's bad for everybody.

During our initial interview, shortly before birthing her second daughter, Laura imagines the damaging consequences that her elder daughter would likely endure should Laura follow conventional mothering practices:

> It would be like cutting off her legs; it would be like binding her feet. Because of who I am, and because I want to give her the freedom to be, every night that I put her to bed, I rock her, give her a bottle and rock her. And she's a year and a half; she doesn't need a bottle anymore.
>
> And I sing *The Flirtations Lullaby* which goes [singing]: "You can be anybody that you want to be. You can love whomever you will. You can travel the world where your heart leads, and you know I will love you still. You can live by yourself. You can gather friends around. You can choose one special one; but the only measure of your words and your deeds will be the love you leave behind when you are gone."

Laura stops singing for a moment to clarify that she likes this song because "It specifically addresses gender roles" and then carries on singing the last lines of the song: "Some girls grow up strong and bold. Some boys are quiet and kind. Some race on ahead, some follow behind. Some grow in their own space and time." She concludes by explaining the hope she attaches to the song's message and to the shared tender moments between herself and her daughter that are generated by singing, saying, "It's just wonderful and it's my hope for her. To mother the way like Betty Crocker wouldn't give her those chances. It would be awful for her and it would also be awful for me. It wouldn't be true to me."

Clearly Laura, like Beverly, Neire, and Jody, views the expectations placed on women and children within mainstream motherhood to be limiting and damaging. She uses the language of enslavement, victimization, and abuse to describe the negative implications of patriarchal motherhood in her critique. Laura also recognizes that she has the ability to mother differently than the prescribed standard of mothering she so readily depicts, and easily acknowledges that mothering any other way than her own would not be "true" to her.

Other feminist mothers concur with her analysis of conventional conceptions of motherhood and with Laura's critical portrayal of the stereotypical mother being strongly associated with concepts of the ideal wife signified, in this case, by the Betty Crocker stereotype from the 1950s. They, too, critique and dispute this restrictive and damaging construct of motherhood, know mothering in this way can be contested and challenged and, I suggest, would likely fully agree with Andrea O'Reilly's assertion that "Mothering does not require self erasure."[136] For these women, having a feminist consciousness and politic entails being critical of patriarchy and its influence on people's everyday lives, including the work of and relations associated with mothering. And since they all believe that their autonomy, agency, and ability to make positive decisions for themselves and their children are based on their feminist understanding of the world, and that they understand mothering—like all elements of their lives—to be both personal and political, each woman believes her mothering is a political act. It is to this understanding that I now turn.[137]

Feminist Mothering is a Political Act

> When I became a conscious feminist, I realized that raising children alternatively was, in fact, a very political act. Everything we do with others certainly has political implications.[138]

As plainly articulated in the previous section addressing the institution of motherhood and also in the above quote by Shar, these feminist mothers understand both the enormous pressure placed on women to conform to mainstream motherhood and the significant consequences for any rebellion against that ideal. They are fully cognizant of the distinction made by Rich between the "two meanings of motherhood" that appear to be "superimposed" on one another, and of the ways in which women are regulated and expected to conform to an ideal of mothering that does not necessarily reflect their experiences.[139]

They are also well aware of the pressure to follow current models of intensive and sacrificial mothering, theorized by Hays and O'Reilly respectively, and of the impossibility of meeting these mythical ideals. They identify the social expectations, such as the nuclear family and the stay-at-home mother, that are endorsed and supported in society, and recognize the significant consequences of being marked a "bad mother" for not meeting the criteria presented by so called experts and authorities. They acknowledge other confining aspects of motherhood, such as the isolation and abnegation of mothers, and the negative effects these have on women and children, citing, in particular, how girls are expected and taught to be enslaved to the demands of their fathers and husbands and how internalizing these beliefs damage mother's self-esteem.

Building on their feminist understanding of the gendered power dynamics inherent in patriarchy, of the intricate interconnection of the personal and political and of the right of all people to personal autonomy and choice, they recognize that patriarchal motherhood is not completely totalitarian, nor fixed. They also know from their own knowledge and experience that motherhood is not entirely oppressive. Believing in the importance of praxis—the ability of putting one's understanding into action—they are committed to resisting the damaging requirements of motherhood by redefining mothering for themselves and their families in ways that are more meaningful and fit more comfortably with their feminist worldview.

Again drawing from interviews, this time with Jody, Kim, and May, I illustrate some of the ways in which feminism helps these women recognize their need to engage in a practice of parenting that fits more comfortably with their vision and philosophy of mothering than the ones stipulated by the institution of motherhood. Jody, a separated mother of two teenagers, is very clear about the influence of her feminism on her critique of motherhood and on her awareness that she has the capacity to approach her own mothering in her own way when she says:

> I'm separated because I'm a feminist [laughter] and because I've challenged some of the ways I was supposed to be constructed in this "Motherhood." And I went against those knowing I can't live within that parameter [and saying to my husband] "Either you understand that and come along with me or this isn't going to work."
>
> And with my children, it's about who I am, so I hope they gain those strengths about who I am. But at the same time, there's kind of a paradox with what you're supposed to be, what's out there and says what you're supposed to be. And trying to challenge that in a different way and realizing where you fall into certain things and then challenge them again for yourself. And hoping that your kids pick up on that, like when they ask particular questions, you answer them as honestly as you can.
>
> To me, that's half the battle, so that they know that I'm not trying to make things up. I can talk about the pain or the differences and not be ashamed of that, but rather embrace that. And when I fail, I can say that I failed when I had bouts of anger [laughter] and that anger is normal, and talk about how to use it.

Being feminist, for Jody and for the rest of these women, entails being critical of the expectations placed on them as mothers and bringing their feminism into their relationships with their children, and with their partners should they be partnered. Each woman recognizes the influence she has on the life of her child/ren and the responsibility she has as a mother to the next generation.

Kim told me during an interview in 1996 that because her mothering is inherently political, she is committed to raising her two young sons—then aged two and four years—with a feminist awareness of social injustice. Kim's feminism also informs her relationship with her male partner of 17 years and the father of their sons. By deciding to live common-law rather than marry at this time, Kim and her partner model an alternative way of living for their children and for others. Kim told me she was living her politics in a way that helped support the argument that gays and lesbians are legitimate couples:[140]

> When we were first together there was pressure on us to get married and I resisted it because of my feminism. I think by not getting married and living common-law we provide an alternative. We provide gay and lesbian couples with an argument "If they can get benefits and they're not married, why can't two women?"

Kim was also optimistic about being able to teach her sons how to be aware and critical of the world, noting that she often talked with them about sexism, heterosexism, and the importance of democracy and non-violence. Although her sons were still relatively young at the time, she taught them about various forms of injustice in the world by telling them, for example, about the importance of respecting women and people's diverse sexuality. Her feminism is evident in her relationship with her children, particularly in her commitment to teaching them how to be aware and critical of various forms of oppression:

> My mothering is absolutely a political act. It's the personal is political. You know, trying to teach my sons my values, my feminist values by doing, by being. And also to teach them the ability to criticize the world and not to just take it for what it is.
>
> Like, I tell my boys, "Sports are great, but I'm encouraging you to do this because it's good for you and healthy and there're lots of wonderful things about it." Right now it's too early for this, but when they get older, [I'll likely tell them]

"It's also competitive, it often excludes women and you know, there're all kinds of other problems." So hopefully I'll be able to teach them how to look at a situation and not just take it. To give them tools to criticize is what I see the political side of it. It's to bring it into the next generation.

My heartache would be around them not getting it somehow and treating the women in their lives really lousy. And that's the biggest challenge I see for myself as a feminist and a mother of my kids. I hope like hell that they absorb my values and that they don't, as they become adolescents, reject them all and become skinheads or something; but skinheads wouldn't take them 'cause they're Jewish, so that's an upside [laughter].

Other feminist mothers are sensitive to the influence they have in the lives of their children and the role feminism plays in their mothering. May, for example, acknowledges that her mothering is informed by her feminism. Aware of her role in the development of the next generation, she consciously mothers her two daughters "so that they can make their own choices" and pays close attention to her relationship with them and to the values she teaches and models for them.

May was born and raised in Guyana in the mid 1950s and moved to Canada in her 20s with her Euro-Canadian husband. At the time of our second interview in the summer of 1997, she had just separated from her spouse and father of their two teenage biracial daughters. While we sat together sharing a cool drink at her dining room table, May reflected on how her feminism informs her approach to raising her daughters and on how she is making a significant contribution to the world and to social change through her feminist mothering:

To be a mother to me is a big thing. As I say, you have the generation in your hand. And we can do a lot to shape that, regardless of whatever is out there; you can still make a big impact being a mother.

I really believe in mothering. It's a feminist thing. It's a very special power that women have that we should not lose

> sight of. We're raising children that will take our place, and they're gonna shape that world. And what we put out in them, that is what they're gonna put out. We have to be careful what we teach them. We can help them to think critically on different issues by presenting them with all these ideas.
>
> I'm raising kids for the next generation. I'm trying to give them a new sense of what it is to be women. I'm trying to give them some understanding of where oppression is, and to encourage them to always seek justice; to fight for that kind of thing, and truth, and so on. The way I'm raising them is to resist the current structure, even in the schools. Like telling them, "You don't feel the teachers are being fair, so speak out, but do it in a respectful way. Just speak out."

May shares her understanding and critique of patriarchy, sexism, racism, and other forms of discrimination with her daughters, noting her commitment to refusing to accept and also opposing the social expectations placed on girls and women, particularly to become mothers and to become mothers in service of patriarchy:

> I am not raising my kids in that same mould. I am resisting that set traditional, patriarchal way of raising kids. To be girls, to be neat and tidy and whatever it is that girls gotta be. I think part of our nature as women may be we are the child bearers, but that is not the primary thing. There's so much more we can offer; it's a choice, to have kids or not. And I want my daughters to know that.

Like the other feminist mothers, May understands the pressure to conform to a patriarchal model of motherhood and the consequences for non-compliance. And like the other feminist mothers, she believes there is room for resistance, invention, renewal, and reform within its structure. Rather than acquiesce to the expectations associated with the institution of motherhood, she reconstructs her mothering by actively resisting elements of its confining structure and creates different ways of mothering:

> It is hopefully true that the strategy of feminist mothering can bring about social change because it just takes one person to start something. It is a political act, because the personal is political, that's the thing.

Concluding Remarks

Unlike some second wave feminists who considered motherhood to be inescapably oppressive, these particular self-identified feminist mothers are conscious of the difference between social prescriptions of motherhood and their personal experiences of mothering and intentionally attempt to become the mothers they want to be. Their feminism enables them to uncover, reject, and reform its restrictive and damaging aspects, along with its negative repercussions for women and children. As such, they engage in feminist praxis and feminist intervention practices of dealing with the tension between their own image of mothering and the socially prescribed institution of motherhood and the messiness of revising, reforming, and reconstructing mothering for themselves and their families.

By separating the possibility of autonomous, mother-centred mothering from the harsh demands required by patriarchal institutionalized motherhood, mothering becomes a site of feminist political activism where they consciously bring together their feminism and mothering to trouble and contest the patriarchal institution of motherhood and to practice alternative approaches to mothering through their parenting that empower them and their children. Their experiences and knowledge of motherhood support the evaluation made by other feminist researchers that feminist mothering is a "process of resistance that entails making different choices about how one wants to practice mothering."[141]

The following two chapters delve more deeply into how these feminist mothers engage in the political act of feminist mothering. The next chapter specifically explores how they consciously integrate their feminism into their parenting to reclaim their maternal power and to alleviate some of the ways institutionalized patriarchal motherhood regulates and restrains mothers and their mothering. I now turn to this example of feminist political activism that is still not that well understood.[142]

CHAPTER 3

Matroreform: Breaking the Rules of Motherhood

Nothing is ever benign. I feel huge amounts of responsibility as a feminist. If I see something then I am compelled to act. I can't be silent. So it's heavy, it's huge, overwhelming at times. And then I think, "Would I have it any other way?" And I think "NO! I'm so alive."[143]

While the last chapter addressed the ways in which feminist mothers understand feminism, the institution of motherhood and how their feminist mothering is a political act, the purpose of this chapter is to look more closely at the complicated positioning of feminist mothers and the ways in which they navigate the tensions between the social (and their internalized) expectations of motherhood and their own understandings of feminism and parenting.

I begin, in the first section, by exploring how mothers engage in feminist praxis as they move from a critical understanding of the institution of motherhood that is informed by their feminism to a conscious practice of resisting some of its damaging elements (for themselves and their children) and parenting in ways that are informed by and respect their own experience and knowledge. In the second section, I critically examine how feminist mothers understand, trouble, and resist the dynamics of power and control in mother/child relationships prescribed by the institution of motherhood to demonstrate how they implement their feminist praxis to engage in a practice of mothering that is more in tune with their feminist worldview and goals of parenting that respects the human rights and autonomy of their children. In the last section of the chapter, I argue that the feminist praxis of these feminist mothers ensures that they break the rules of patriarchal motherhood and also practice matroreform: the conscious process of (re) claiming mothering power by establishing alternative rules and practicing customs different to those (previously) prescribed by others.[144]

Contesting the Institution of Motherhood: Defining and Re-creating mothering

> My feminism has been an evolutionary process and so has my mothering. I couldn't be a mother in the way that society has defined for me to be a mother where there are these duties; this is where you begin and where it ends. God! What a thankless waste of time. The prescribed way is so empty. I couldn't do it under those conditions or under those terms; not at all.[145]

All of the feminist mothers I spoke with understand motherhood to be a patriarchal and demeaning institution that, while a part of society and a reality in their lives, need not be completely ubiquitous or absolutely tyrannical. Each woman saw and created opportunities within her feminist mothering to confront, defy, and reform elements of the institution she found repressive and harmful. Believing mothering to be a site of empowerment for both herself and her child/ren meant she was able to take on the messy work of shaping her mothering to more readily reflect her vision of mothering.[146]

To further explore how mothers practice feminist praxis in parenting, I draw upon interviews with three specific women, Andrea, Willow, and Deb, who each discuss how they rely upon their feminism and their experiences of mothering to create some distance from the regulations of institutionalized motherhood and how they reshape motherhood in ways that are compatible with their critique of motherhood and with their vision of mothering. No longer strictly confined by the social prescriptions of motherhood, mothering for these women is a political site of feminist activism where they engage in self-reflexive subjectivity which is informed by their feminism to deal with the contradictions and tensions between the prescribed ideal of motherhood and their own vision of mothering. Andrea, for example, engages in a process of analyzing, critiquing, and refusing to give in to the internalization of the dominant social definition of stay-at-home mother. Willow defies heterosexist demands of motherhood and creates a family of choice to support her vision of mothering. And Deb, quoted above, invents a more subversive practice of mothering for herself and her son by becoming a mother in her own image and developing a relationship with him based on respecting his human rights.

Andrea and I met at her home in a middle-class neighbourhood where she and her male partner of ten years lived with and raised their one-and-a-half-year-old child. Upon moving back to Winnipeg a few months after the homebirth of their daughter in Toronto, Andrea's identity quickly changed from full-time employee and graduate student to stay-at-home mother. As she shifted from contributing financially to the household to being financially dependent on her husband and his home-based business, Andrea spent most of that first year and a half struggling with her new identity as a stay-at-home mom. Despite the fact that she is now at peace with her situation, Andrea found the most difficult aspect of this transition was coming to understand and respond to the tension between what she knew about mothering from her own experiences and the messages about motherhood she had internalized since childhood:

> At this point in my life, I am, for all intents and purposes, a stay-at-home mom with a very part-time job. And where my identity fits into that is a really big struggle for me. I'm struggling with my identity as someone who makes no financial contribution to my household and who I am as an individual compared to the Betty Crocker stay-at-home mom stereotype.

> As I said, between what I know intellectually and my ability to reject the image of what a stay-at-home mom is and wanting on some level to embrace certain aspects of that, and wanting others to reject other aspects wholeheartedly.

Andrea's struggle with her shifting identity and the tension she experienced between the pressure to conform to conventional notions of the stay-at-home mom and her desire to mother according to her own beliefs was a discussion we returned to during our second interview which took place about six months after the first in 1997. Andrea explains how, with the assistance of a feminist friend, she was able to make it through her self-defined "mini-crisis" and fashion an appropriate way of mothering that coincides with her feminist ethos and vision of mothering that rejects the role of wife, while embracing the role of mother:

> And that was a tremendous click for me. I hadn't recognized that what society talks about when they talk about mother is also what they talk about with wife; that for the rest of the world, those two things are intertwined and that, if you are a mother, you *should* be a wife. First and very importantly you must be married. And you would also, as part of your mothering duties, do things like the laundry and the cleaning and the cooking and whatever else to take care of the home.
>
> That wasn't what mothering was about for me. And it took my friend pointing this out for me to understand that, in fact, my perception of mothering was really different than what the world's concept is, what society's concept is.

Andrea finds it impossible to conform to the socially prescribed mould of the stay-at-home mother that demands she take on the duties of "wife" because she separates these two identities for herself. Whilst Andrea is married, she does not view herself as a wife, noting, "In no way, shape, or form do I define myself as a wife. I recognize that that's what I am, technically speaking, and I don't have a problem with the fact that I am, officially, a 'wife.' But that's not who I am. That's not what

I do." For Andrea, mothering is about being at home with her daughter, playing, learning, and getting out in the world, and not about the wifely duties of keeping house and baking cookies, for instance.

Between our first and second interview, Andrea gave up her part-time job, enabling her to redefine mothering in a way that allowed her to feel good and to more fully become the mother she preferred to be:

> I've made peace with the concept of being a stay-at-home mom. I gave up a job I was not happy in and have been thrilled ever since. For me, it was very much an intellectual/emotional issue that I had to be able to say "I choose this, that it's okay, and that I can make it be whatever I want it to be. But it doesn't have to be what anyone else says it's going to be."

In rejecting the role of wife while embracing the role of mother, Andrea denounces and severs the connection of these two roles and creates a practice of mothering that honours her desire to stay at home with her daughter and also contests the harmful elements of "the Betty Crocker stay-at-home mom stereotype." This revelation was not simple, quick, or without emotional distress and anxiety. With the help of her feminist friend she was able to be critical of the pressures to conform to a patriarchal ideal of mothering that caused her discomfort and tension, and as a result, Andrea has reformed mothering in a way that is true to her own vision, grounded in her own experiences, and makes her "happy while doing it."

Willow, too, uses her feminist analysis and perspective to redefine her mothering. We met twice in 1998, first in Willow's home and then again in a university classroom to talk about feminist mothering. On both of those occasions, Willow's 10-year-old daughter was close by, reading, listening, and, at times, joining our conversation. Willow and I spent considerable time talking about the conscious decision she made a decade before, at age 27, to birth and raise her daughter alone.

As a child, Willow suffered substantial emotional, psychological, and physical abuse from both of her parents and describes herself as an "orphan who was raised by nobody." Growing up without a mother as a role model, she developed an ability to question everything, including "how families are constructed, the rules and regulations around mothering, and what mothering might look like if done differently." She also realized that she "had to divorce [her] original family" and "rebuild the family from the inside out."

Willow describes her peer group during the late 1980s as "feminist and pretty much lesbian" and not at all supportive of her decision to become pregnant and parent a child because, as she notes, "they were not having babies at the time and it wasn't something they knew how to support in any way." Although conceiving and having a child were outside conventional practices for lesbians at the time, Willow nevertheless followed her desire and need to be a mother. Already estranged from her family and misunderstood by her friends and community, Willow bore the cost of losing her peer group and became isolated and alone in her pregnancy and for the first few years of her daughter's life. Through this difficult time of birthing and mothering, Willow had what she calls "flashbacks" to her own experiences as a child, and came to understand how she had missed bonding with her own mother in her childhood.

For Willow, the act of birthing and solely raising a child meant making the difficult "conscious decisions and actions of dissidence" and engaging in a deliberate act of resistance to dominant conceptions of motherhood and its applicable practices of mothering. Willow explained to me how the acts of birthing and solely raising a child without any connection to a man are mindful actions of resistance to dominant conceptions of motherhood and practices of "good" mothering:

> I mean basically, in order to do this, I broke all the rules and I went about this in the most conscious manner that I knew at that time. Although, to be honest with you, because my

> consciousness has changed I'd probably go about it differently now. But back ten years ago, I broke all the rules by making a choice to be a mother. Nobody told me I had to be a mother because I was married or that I had to get married in order to do this. I made choices for myself.
>
> So in the late '80s and '90s there are particular ways that you're supposed to be a mother and they include either be married to somebody who is relatively wealthy and can allow you to stay home, or put the kid in daycare at the age of six weeks, or as soon as your maternity leave runs out, and pay attention to the money issue more than to anything else and run out to work. And I did not do that.
>
> I did not let myself be subjugated, as it were, by men. I'm not married now, and I never have been and no man ever called the shots in my home. Nor did a man ever support me in any way. So that is really breaking the rules in the patriarchy. It is clearly the most holistic act of resistance that I have ever done and the most difficult.

Mothering for Willow is not only about birthing and mothering a child; it is also about reclaiming her ability to bond with other human beings, breaking the rules of institutionalized motherhood, and challenging and reforming patriarchal constructions of the family. By consciously choosing to become a mother and to raise her daughter alone, Willow experienced both self-described hardship and great pleasure. Wanting to raise her child without the interference of others and without the financial means to do so, Willow lived on social assistance for a few years. Finding herself without enough money to make ends meet, she often bartered with others, exchanging child care or reading or singing lessons for goods and services. Qualified as a certified teacher helped Willow decide to educate her daughter at home because she believed that home schooling was the best option for her daughter's development at the time.

When her daughter was eight years old and entered the public school system after expressing a desire and demonstrating a need to do so, Willow returned to part-time work and also became a member of an "alternative" or "chosen family" where she and several individuals who weren't biologically related to each other agreed to support and care for each other. Most of her new family members were women with children; some were feminist, while others were not.

During our second interview, Willow, then 37 years old, told me how she had recently found it difficult to deal with some of the behaviour of her pre-teenage daughter. She was worried that should her daughter's behaviour escalate that someone may call Child and Family Services to intervene, fanning her fear, like that of most mothers, of having her daughter removed from their home. Being aware of her marginalized status as a poor, single, lesbian mother and her rather radical approach to parenting, Willow decided to call upon her chosen family for support:

> I went to these people and I said, "I need some help. And if it isn't you, it's nobody, because there's nobody else for this child to perceive to be her family and I need help." So I said, "I'm sorry, but you've got to help." And they did, because I demanded it [laughter].
>
> I've also had to remind them that what I want here is to be backed and I don't want any judgment or any blame or anything else like that. I want them to take responsibility as well, because I can't do this by myself anymore.
>
> I am inventing it as I go along because I had no mother in the first place, and no mothering. And my community is tremendously important to me at this time because I can't possibly do this by myself.

With the help of one particular family member, who was also a feminist mother, Willow was able to effectively deal with her daughter's unwanted behaviour. Together the two women shared the parental responsibilities of caring for Willow's daughter for a few months, allowing her to live with her other feminist mother for a few days or, on occasion, for up to a couple of weeks at a time. This arrangement helped to simultaneously create much needed space for both Willow and her daughter and to ensure that they remained positively connected. Living within the same neighbourhood meant the mothers and daughter were able to be in touch with each other on a regular basis through family meetings to discuss and work through the situation. Within four months Willow and her daughter were living together again, and the unwanted behaviour had been dealt with in a loving and effective manner. Willow and her daughter continued to seek out the other feminist mother whenever they felt they needed her help and support.

In creating an alternative feminist model of mothering by expanding her family to include another feminist mother, Willow is able to address the needs of her daughter while keeping their relationship intact. She is also able to create a practice of mothering that does not replicate the heterosexual nuclear family, or intensive/sacrificial motherhood prescribed by patriarchy. Through successfully creating her own solution to her daughter's challenging behaviour, which she believed would most likely have been considered a major concern by others, and their unique situation as a family, Willow was able to keep herself from being labelled an "unfit" mother and from possibly losing her daughter to the state through Child and Family Services or another similar social agency. Continually inventing approaches to parent in ways that meet her needs also means that while painful and lonely at times, Willow enjoys a level of "freedom and strength" that she says she would not have experienced had she conformed to a patriarchal model of family or to the standard method of mothering when dealing with a "problem" daughter.

Contesting the institution of motherhood is undoubtedly a tricky and lengthy endeavour that requires various strategies and actions in multiple locations. Some feminist mothers, like 35-year-old Deb, find using their socially sanctioned position as mother within the institution of motherhood to be an effective tactic to challenge patriarchal notions of mothering and motherhood. Deb, the heterosexual mother of an eight-year-old boy, speaks openly about her strategy of using feminist mothering as a significant site to contest and resist patriarchy:

> Someone can look at me on the surface and go, "Okay, there's a woman who's chosen to be a mother. Good, patriarchy likes that. Good, good." They don't have a clue! I have the ability to transform what I perceive the role to be, to take it on, to claim it, and to just create it. I'm a mother in my own image in the absence of a role model, or someone who's telling me how to do it. I guess the thing that I was amazed at was just how wonderful I find my experience of mothering to be in a non-patriarchal way.

While Deb knows that she is considered by others to be a "good" mother because she meets its conventional criteria of being in a monogamous, long-term common-law relationship with the father of their child, she also recognizes that she uses this perception of who she is as a mother to reform motherhood by inventing mothering for herself, as she notes above, and to engage in a relationship with her son that does not replicate one that demands she teach him patriarchal lessons. Deb is "subversively resistant" in her approach to mothering, noting:

> On the one hand, I'm fulfilling this ideal of what women do; we procreate, we nurture, we produce future workers for the future society. Yet, on the other, I've done all those things and so much more. You have no idea what you're going to be up against in the next ten to fifteen years from this child as he unleashes himself on the world. It's subversively resistant because on the surface it's very much, "Oh yeah, she's very much a mother. Okay, we know what's going on with her in her little household." And in reality, it's you don't even have a clue.

Like Andrea and Willow cited earlier, Deb finds it "really liberating to step away from the conventional and invent as you go along," and admits, as do the others, that there is a downside to feminist mothering which "can be terribly isolating and lonely." Trying to identify and seek out like-minded women and children has been a challenge for Deb, and she speaks of "grieving the lack of community" and being in the depths of isolation because she does not have a community that "recognizes concurrently [her] feminism and mothering and the connection between the two." Within mothering circles she is often isolated as a feminist because she refuses to engage in the "typical gender socialization and instrumental expressive behaviour" and "raising a male child to be a non-aggressive, non-competitive athlete is a huge threat to everybody's sense of masculinity." She censors herself, "picking and choosing how feminist [she's] going to be during the mom talk with all the other moms" as she waits for her son after school because she feels "it's not always safe" for her or for her son if she is openly feminist at all times. Her son, too, experiences isolation and criticism and sometimes returns from school to tell her "I'm not fitting in" because he's being ostracized or bullied.

Deb admits to feeling some guilt during these moments, yet upon scrutinizing what that guilt is about and thinking about possibly mothering in a non-feminist manner, she always comes to the same conclusion that she "wouldn't mother in any other way." Like the other feminist mothers, Deb is adamant in her continual choice to parent as a feminist, noting, "This isn't just about me and this kid. It's something I do for all of us. It's not innocuous. Whether I do this as a feminist or in any other way, how I mother has a profound impact on my son and the world in which he lives, and will continue to live. It's hugely political. I don't see that society identifies it as such, but I certainly do."

All of the mothers I spoke with are aware of the disparaging gaze of others—whether teachers, other family members, strangers, or agencies working for the state.[147] Deb provides an example of constantly having to deal with judgmental authority figures, in this case of a year-long battle with a kindergarten teacher who would not deal with the issue of her son being ostracized by the girls in his kindergarten class when he wanted to play in the kitchen with them because, as Deb says, she "refused to hammer and poke and prod him down into a box to meet the gender role expectations of the teacher." Willow, too, acknowledges the power of the gaze of others, particularly that of social service agencies to take her daughter away from her during the difficult time when she called upon her chosen family to assist in preventing her from being labelled an "unfit" mother by the state. Andrea's self-described struggle with the overlapping socially prescribed roles and duties of wife and mother also speaks to the influence of the patriarchal gaze upon mothers to relinquish authority to others because they have never gained, or subsequently lost, confidence in their own values and abilities to parent.

Although conflict and tension are part of feminist mothering, all of the women I interviewed, to use Deb's language, create "mothering in their own image" and craft a mothering practice for themselves and their children that is informed by their feminist interrogation and contestation of the institution of motherhood and their desire and will to parent differently than the model offered.

As noted in Chapter Two, this group of feminist mothers is acutely aware of the influence they have in the lives of their children and the influence their children (will) have on the world. In understanding that the relationships that all mothers have with their children—whether based on a feminist politic or not—these particular parents are critically aware of, and attentive to, their interaction with their children and the values they demonstrate, model, and teach their children. Furthermore, they interact with their children in their mother/child relationships in ways that are based upon their feminist principles and therefore do not replicate patriarchal values and structures based on hierarchies and domination. By troubling and resisting the dynamics of power and control in mother/child relationships prescribed by the institution of motherhood they engage in a practice of mothering that respects the human rights and autonomy of their children.

Engaging in Non-Hierarchal Relationships

> For me, it's huge to accept the responsibility of my choice to become a mother and to parent. I refuse to take complete responsibility for who my child is. My responsibility is to give him the tools, to provide a safe, nurturing, warm environment in which he can grow, thrive, learn, and love. But I'm not responsible, in the end, for who he is or who he will be. That's him. That's the beauty of it all. It only makes sense; there's no way my parents would take responsibility for who I am today. There's a certain amount of responsibility for your choice, but not responsibility for who this person is. That is different from the patriarchal blaming of mothers for their children's behaviour and outcome.

To consider how mothers acknowledge the influence they have on the lives of their children and how their commitment to engaging in respectful relationships with their children is an element of their feminist parenting, I draw upon interviews with Deb, quoted above, Jackie, and Carol. I begin with a description of how Deb respects herself and her son by mothering in her own image and how she has developed a relationship with her son based on her awareness of her power as an adult, and a mother, and on the need as a feminist to respect her son's human rights. I then turn to Jackie, who demonstrates how her commitment to reducing violence against women informs how she raises her son, and in particular how she deals with violence and sexism both outside and within the home. Carol offers further insight into the positive outcomes that can occur, even in difficult situations, by developing open, honest, and respectful relationships with children.

Like the other feminist mothers, Deb is extremely conscious of the influence she has in her child's life—particularly of the power she has as an adult and a mother in their relationship—and the possible damage she could inflict upon her son:

> I can crush this child's spirit if I wanted to, and that makes me sad. I'm not that way inclined, but I'm aware of his trust

> in me, of his love for me, and his respect for me. We're still in the sort of honeymoon phase where I'm the pseudo goddess and I could really, really, hurt him if I wanted to. I could really screw with his head or with his being by damaging him. I don't ever think of children as being lesser people; I think of them as being just little people.

Deb believes her son "came into the world with a set of human rights" that she has fought very hard to maintain and has also been criticized for by others. For instance, she has been accused of "robbing him of his childhood and his innocence, and, therefore, hurting him in some way because [she] accepts and respects that he has power in [her] family and in [her] relationship with him." Deb rejects this assessment of her parenting, saying, "the hurt comes by denying him power" and that her feminism helps her "determine the principles, approach, and language" she practices in her relationship with her son and her parenting:

> When you talk about empowerment and non-violence and non-aggression, they are not exclusive to mothering. In fact, those are not words you find in mothering manuals or parenting books; these are words that belong to feminist movement and principles from which I parent. And I've got no role models out there to model this feminist mothering for me, or to assure me how this is going to go. And so, I'm winging it, trusting that it has to be better than what the patriarchy has to offer. But it involves taking risks in mothering, doing some unconventional things and being wary and ever cognizant of the social sanctions for my son.

Always mindful of the particular kind of relationship she wants to engage in with her son, Deb speaks openly and frankly with her son about the power dynamics and structure of their relationship:

> It started at birth with my son. I've always taken pains to not just have this relationship with him, but to be able to take a step back and talk about the kind of relationship we

> have with each other. Like asking him, "When I did this, I was feeling that and how did you feel about that? Didn't that suck?" Or, "Are we okay?" I wanted us to talk about things on a different level.
>
> He's got a consciousness about relationships, even at age eight, that I have to suggest he'll carry with him for the rest of his life. So I'm hoping he'll be one of those rare males who will be able to share and feel safe in doing so; that it's not such a huge risk for him because he's always been able to talk about his feelings, to take a step back away from his feelings and look at the larger dynamic and who's getting hurt and why and what purpose does it serve. That's one of the goods about the power; it's using it responsibly and sharing it and I'm more than willing to do so with him.

When Deb and her son have disagreements and lively discussions, Deb is vigilant in ensuring that their exchanges are respectful. Under her guidance, they have each learned to watch for negative behaviour or condescending attitudes, to notice when they sense power shift between them, and to note when they feel disrespected. Deb explains, "While we aren't always able to mediate those things in the moment, we do come back to a whole process that we are both engaged in." She is amazed that they are able to have spirited discussions where her son "won't let go of his power," where she "doesn't lose hers," and where they come to an understanding that while they may not agree, they continue to respect each other.

Being consciously aware of injustice caused by patriarchy, racism, homophobia, ageism, class bias, and capitalism, as well as the violence that often accompanies these interlocking social systems, informs the parenting of all of these feminist mothers. Deb is adamant about talking with her son about violence and has done so since he was a very young age. To give her son a sense of the implications of violence, she has "had to give him some really gory, graphic, and concrete information about what death means." Because she has a "positive outlook about death that is very natural because we're all going to die" and believes that "we all have the right to die peaceably by non-violent means," Deb had a series of ongoing conversations with her son over several months about death and violence. Even though he was scared and went through a period of realizing that his mother was eventually going to die, Deb thought the conversations were necessary for him to understand why she doesn't condone violence, why she's a pacifist and why it is important to her to have him not engage in violent behaviour. She acknowledges it meant, at times, that they were "uncomfortable and got scared, or were talking about some things that weren't necessarily pleasant and were pretty heavy for kids," yet she believes these intense and deep conversations "benefit him and society."

Jackie, a Métis, heterosexual, 41-year-old, single mother is also concerned about preventing violence in the lives of women and children and speaks often with her 11-year-old son about the damage it causes in their lives and in other people's lives. When Jackie and I met in the spring and late summer of 1997, she reflected upon the personal impact the 1989 Montreal massacre has on her awareness of violence against women, on how she is particularly sensitive to sexist violence, and on the fear she often feels as a feminist.[148] Well aware of the prevalence and challenges of dealing with sexist violence inside and outside the home, Jackie remarks, "It's so much a part of this world and even at home, it's something I constantly try to work on."

To explain the influence of sexism in the life of her son, she describes how she witnessed the sexist terms her son had learned from his peer group who "use the words 'slut,' 'bag,' and other derogatory words to describe or refer to girls and women." She shared an incident that had occurred the previous week when her son "had been playing too roughly with a girl in the local swimming pool and had called her down for being weak." Together, Jackie and her son talked about how his aggressive behaviour was hurtful, not only to the girl but also to him. She reminded him about his recent hurtful experience of being called "welfare boy" while playing outside by a hockey teammate because they didn't live in the same affluent neighbourhood. Jackie spoke with her son about his sexist and aggressive behaviour, "drawing parallels between the pain he felt from the aggressive remarks made by the boy about his class and the hurt feelings the girl probably felt from his remarks about her gender."

Rather than blame her son or the other boy in these situations, Jackie makes an effort to explain and teach her son "about the damage and wrongs of aggression, sexism, and classism." Being highly conscious of the social and peer pressure placed on her son to be aggressive, Jackie sometimes struggles with her decision of allowing him to play in organized hockey, which he is passionate about. The tension around this decision is partly due to the non-violent and non-competitive values she was taught as a child by her Aboriginal grandmother and aunties and partly due to her critical feminist analysis of the values of violence taught in hockey.

During our second interview in her home early one summer evening, Jackie talked about the complexity and challenges of being a single mother on the meagre income provided by social assistance which she had been on for the past three years since the sudden and unexpected death of her common-law partner and father of their son. At that difficult time, Jackie decided to leave her job as a social worker and stay home to help her young school-age son recover from the loss of his father and to not lose his way in his studies. While she felt isolated and restrained without adequate funds to purchase a car or a computer for her son to use for his schoolwork, they developed a close and respectful relationship and her son did very well in school. During that second interview, Jackie was also feeling particularly anxious about the current legislative changes that had recently forced her—as the mother of a child over five years—to reenter the labour force.[149]

Feeling unable to return to a career in social work because she found the work to be too emotionally draining, Jackie had just begun training to become an accounting clerk. Now that she was working part-time and taking courses, Jackie no longer had the same kind of time to help her son with his homework and felt badly that his marks had slipped from straight A grades. Being as resourceful as possible, Jackie continues to engage in a respectful relationship that values non-violence and where she "patiently listens to and supports him with his homework, discusses—without judgment—the choices that he makes in his language and behaviour, and gets him equipment and bursaries for his sports."

Like Deb and Jackie, who value speaking openly and honestly with their children, Carol, a 58-year-old heterosexual, single mother of a biological 19-year-old son, an adoptive mother of a 24-year-old niece, and a social mother to four adult children of a previous male partner, told me that "talking with everything out in the open" is crucial to her feminist mothering and her relationships with her six children. Carol and I sat together in her living room one August afternoon in 2005, while a contract worker repaired the basement and her teenage son slept upstairs after working a late-night shift. Carol was eager to talk and started our conversation by saying, "I just wanted to tell you this one thing 'cause the whole premise is feminist and this happened because of their feminist upbringing." Carol proceeded to anxiously relay an alarming incident that had occurred seven years before, when her adopted daughter, then age 17, had secretly been given money and a note inviting her to have a sexual relationship with Carol's boyfriend of four years.

Carol credits her feminist practice of talking directly with all of her children from the time they are a very young age for her daughter's ability to quickly tell her about the situation without fear or humiliation. Over the years she participated in many open and frank talks about inappropriate behaviour with her children, often telling them "if anything happens, you tell Mum, especially if they say, 'don't tell.'" Carol believes her practice of honest communication and the development of trusting relationships with each of her children ensured that her daughter "trusted [her] enough to say something the first time she felt uncomfortable about the way [her] boyfriend took a run at her." The practice of not keeping secrets meant that her boyfriend immediately left when Carol confronted him about his behaviour and told him to "pack his things and get out!" Devastated by this situation, Carol was in counselling for six years where she learned how to deal with her feelings of responsibility and guilt for what happened and to forgive herself for putting her children in a vulnerable situation.

Like other feminist mothers, Carol believes her practice of building a strong relationship with her children that's based on her feminist principles of trust, respect, and open dialogue, and the continual act of sharing knowledge and power with them, empower both mothers and children. In this case, Carol's daughter had the ability to analyze and instantly disclose what was happening and Carol unequivocally accepted her daughter's circumstances and took immediate action to resolve the situation. In Jackie's case, her son felt able to disclose to his mother that he had been called "welfare boy" and the shame he felt in the verbal attack, and Jackie had the capacity to parent in ways that respect him while also honouring her feminism. In Deb's case, both mother and son are empowered to engage in honest reflection on the dynamics of their relationship and the reasons behind the parenting decisions Deb makes for her son. Like all of the other feminist mothers, Deb recognizes the power of her feminist mothering:

> It's been phenomenal when I think about it, to know that I can have that intimate relationship with another human being. It just renews my faith in humankind. It's been very much a product of bringing my feminism to my parenting and this is reflected back. It's not about theory. We can really live like this. It's completely possible. I mean we have it. It's awesome.

> I'm very proud of who I am as a feminist mother, as a feminist, and as a mother. [My son's] certainly given me a sense of my own vision; not just in terms of a mother, but who I am as a person who mothers. It's something I do; it's not the be-all and end-all of my existence, but it gives me the opportunity to be a teacher, a guide, a mentor, a role model, a prophet [laughter]. Through him I've become those things for myself. So instead of being split through this act of mother, I see how I've become mother to myself, to my own identity. And to think I might have missed out on that is frightening. It's just been an awesome journey and will continue to be so.

Matroreform: Breaking the Rules of Motherhood

From the discussion in this and the previous chapter, it is clear that all of the feminist mothers I spoke with are breaking various patriarchal rules intrinsic to the institution of motherhood. Some mothers choose to be single, others decide to be partnered with another woman, and others elect to not be partnered with the biological father of their child/ren. Some mothers withdraw from the labour market and depend upon the state through social assistance rather than on themselves, a partner, or other family members. Other mothers stay at home with their child/ren and refuse to take on the role and responsibility of wife while others are simultaneously students and in the paid labour force.

All mothers also engage in relationships with their children that respect their children's human rights, and consciously work to develop relationships with their children that are open, honest, and non-hierarchal. They are also honest about their own understanding of mothering and their relationships with their children. They have invented and engage in a form of feminist mothering identified by Canadian maternal scholar Andrea O'Reilly that "begins with a recognition that mothers and children benefit when the mother lives her life, and practices mothering, from a position of agency, authority, authenticity, and autonomy."[150] Their particular approach to feminist mothering also "affords a woman a life, a purpose, and identity outside and beyond motherhood,... foregrounds maternal power and confers value to mothering...[and] redefines motherwork as a social and political act that is profoundly political and social."[151]

Like Rich, O'Reilly, and other feminist theorists, these feminist mothers are aware of and consciously contest the oppressive patriarchal institution of motherhood by creating a counter-practice of mothering to the one prescribed. They successfully redefine mothering for themselves and engage in relationships with their children that do not replicate the structures, narratives, or lessons of patriarchal hierarchy within mother/child relationships.[152] As they engage in the active practice and empowering process of incorporating their reflective understandings of patriarchal society and their feminism into their own life experiences, these feminist mothers create meaningful mothering practices for both themselves and their children.

By attending to and sharing their maternal practices and linking them with reflections and understandings of their own relationships with their own mothers/parents as daughters, they actively work to forge strong bonds with their children and to create new feminist mothering practices that both counter and reform those of mainstream motherhood. In doing so, feminist mothers empower themselves and their children by living their lives with authority, agency, and autonomy so central to feminist mothering as articulated by O'Reilly.

According to Canadian feminist psychologist and maternal theorist Gina Wong-Wylie, these feminist mothers engage in matroreform, the empowering process whereby feminist mothers actively claim "motherhood power" by introducing new mothering practices that differ from those of their own mothers and/or the mainstream idealized mother, and work to remove and eliminate "obstacles to self-determination and self-agency." These empowering actions of feminist mothering, according to Wong-Wylie, allow for a "cognitive, affective, behavioral, and spiritual reformation of mothering from within.[153] We also know, from the descriptions in this and the previous chapter of the experiences of feminist mothers who are consciously engaged in the praxis of feminist mothering, that practicing matroreform is paradoxically fraught with tension, complexity, and messiness while also fostering empowerment for mothers and children. Through this active and empowering process of matroreform, feminist mothers along with their children, are reforming and reaffirming feminist motherwork and feminist motherliness in ways that, as noted by O'Reilly, enables them to raise children apart from and against the culture of patriarchy.[154]

CHAPTER 4

Creating Feminist Motherlines: Feminist Mothers and their Daughters

> Attention to maternal narrative links hearing of one's mother's voice as she attempts to challenge patriarchal norms (e.g., mother blame, separation vs. connection) to forging a strong female bond and establishing self-identity. Similarly, the Motherline allows daughters to gain strength from their identities as girls or women as they strengthen the mother-daughter bond through connection.[155]

All of the mothers I interviewed spoke about the significance of their feminism to their understanding and (re)construction of motherhood, and to their commitment to introducing and engaging their children in a feminist worldview that is critical of a patriarchal social system that privileges some folks over others due to social identifiers, such as gender, sex, ethnicity/race, ability, age, social class, and education. They value close relationships with their children, and encourage and involve them in discussions about a range of ideas, realities, and topics. During these open and honest conversations, which are sometimes uncomfortable or painful, mothers and children are candid about their feelings and ideas and learn how to practice respectful and sincere relationships. Together they talk about how the world operates and how they and other people are located within it. While non-feminist mothers certainly have close, frank, and honest discussions with their children, these particular feminist mothers also consciously and deliberately engage their feminism in their everyday lives, including in their relationships with their children and in the parenting decisions they make in their mothering practices.

As I listen to and speak with these women, I am struck by the need to continue sharing and documenting the knowledge and insights of feminist mothering practices; in part to ensure that the practices and strategy of feminist mothering become and remain visible to mothers and their children, and in part to help assure that the difficult and rewarding work of feminist mothering continues to be recognized and recorded as an open and communal feminist strategy for social change.

According to Anglo-American Jewish poet, author, feminist, and Jungian psychologist Naomi Lowinsky, a motherline connects mothers to their female ancestors and helps them to understand how their life stories are linked with previous generations of women in their families and cultures. Motherlines help mothers gain authority in various ways through exposure to an embodied knowledge of mothering, journeying back to their roots through encounters with ancestor women who struggled with challenges of mothering, developing a life-cycle perspective and a worldview of interconnectivity, and having opportunities to reclaim female perspectives that consider how women and men are similar and different.[156]

Maternal scholar Andrea O'Reilly observes through her reading of Toni Morrison and other African American writers and theorists that mothers within the context of African American mothering pass on ancestral memories and ancient properties to their children and others through their motherlines as a way of teaching children the skills of survival and independence and of the importance of remembering one's history and culture. Through their mothers' stories, teachings, mentoring, advocacy, and guidance, children connect with their cultural, familial, and heritage traditions. Daughters develop and nurture their female subjectivity and creativity by identifying with their mothers and relating with their motherline, while sons nurture and sustain themselves in ways that enable them to transcend racism and grow as whole and complete people.[157] Despite the different relationships between a mother and her daughter and a mother and her son, the involvement of a child's mother and the presence of a motherline are crucial to the maturation of all humans regardless of their gender.[158]

Just as motherlines help African American women claim authority and ground their knowledge and practices of mothering, motherlines are equally pertinent to helping feminist mothers reclaim their feminist mothering authority, remain united with a gender-based worldview, ground their own knowledge and the knowledge of other feminist mothers, provide and strengthen a foundation for their ongoing political activism as feminist mothers, and create a legacy of feminist motherwork and feminist mothering practices for themselves and others.[159] And like African American mothers who pass on their African American humanity, history, and culture to their children, feminist mothers draw upon their feminist motherlines to model feminist identities, culture, and strategies for living, including the crucial lessons and skills of critical awareness, survival, and independence for their children and others.[160]

Feminist motherlines afford mothers the opportunity to record, explore, and pass on their own life-cycle perspectives of feminist mothering to their children and other mothers, and the possibility to connect with the feminist mothering practices and motherlines of other feminist mothers.[161] They also ensure a connection with a worldview that is centred on and draws from a feminist gender-based analysis of the world—including parenting—and promises a legacy of feminist mothering practices for others to reflect upon, engage with, critique, learn from, and develop. The process of articulating and recording feminist mothering practices through oral, video, and written communication makes space to share the precious lessons and memories of feminist mothering with mothers and children, while concurrently making visible and validating feminist mothering practices, including the challenges and practical ways in which feminist mothers have chosen to engage the role and responsibility of mothering and how they relate with their young or grown children.[162] As feminist theorist and mother Adrienne Rich notes, "the quality of the mother's life...is her primary bequest to her daughter, because a woman who can believe in herself, who is a fighter, and who continues to create livable space around her, is demonstrating to her daughter that these possibilities exist."[163]

A feminist motherline, then, encapsulates the commitment to, and practice of, acknowledging and articulating the many struggles, pleasures, and conflicts that are involved in and accompany the complex embodied experiences and knowledge/s of feminist motherwork. It also provides a counter-narrative to patriarchal framings of the family that affirm the power of mothers to both live their lives as they see fit and tell their stories as way of self-discovery, empowerment, and ultimately, cultural transformation. When mothers conceive of themselves as agents in their own right, daughters, too, are more likely to claim agency for themselves.

In this chapter I draw upon the experiences and reflections of feminist mothering by both mothers and daughters from interviews I conducted with four feminist mothers over the span of a decade beginning in the mid 1990s, and five of their adult children during the summer and fall of 2007.[164] My discussion is limited to these particular mother/child groupings because they were the folks who were interested and available to speak with me at the time. I was interested in speaking with adult children, given they were more likely to be more independent than younger children and, therefore, more likely to have had time to reflect on their childhood and on their relationships with their mothers.

I begin by introducing and discussing each of the four mother/daughter groupings. Particular attention is given to what feminism means for each mother and for each daughter, as well as how the daughters understand their mothers' feminism and any differences they may perceive between the two. The daughters also reflect upon the influence of their mothers' feminism on their upbringing and on their own understanding of feminism, in addition to the influence their feminist upbringing may have on their own ideas and/or practices of parenting their own children. I conclude by arguing that the reflections made by the daughters of feminist mothers provide evidence of how feminist motherlines are created by both mothers and daughters, and how their collective and insightful understandings continue the act of matroreform which challenges patriarchal norms of motherhood, including those ideals prescribed by intensive and sacrificial mothering, and empowers them to live their lives with authority, agency, and autonomy.

May and Gemma

I begin this section with the mother/daughter pair of May, born in 1955, and her eldest daughter Gemma, born in 1981. May was born in Guyana and raised in a small family with her brother and two sisters primarily by her mother, a farmer and the family's main breadwinner and, to a lesser extent, her father, an underemployed craftsperson. With her high school General Certificate in hand and experience working in the civil service, May married her Euro-Canadian husband and moved to Canada in the mid 1970s in search of better economic opportunities. By the age of 25 she had birthed Gemma, the first of her two daughters, while her husband worked as a teacher on short-term contracts in small towns in Ontario and Manitoba.

May birthed their second daughter two years later and the family eventually settled in the city of Winnipeg where May began working full-time for a non-governmental agency focused on the needs of immigrant women. After sixteen years of marriage, May divorced her spouse and agreed to joint custody of their two teenage daughters. She enjoys being single and thinks "having a partner is like the cream on top of the cake." In other words, while a partner is not necessary to her happiness, being in a relationship may make life a little sweeter.

During our last interview in early 2005, May had been employed for five years as a civil servant for the provincial government addressing human rights, and also working as a freelance writer and reporter. Gemma, then age 23, had been recently married and was making a living as a musician in Winnipeg, while her younger sister, age 21, was finishing her university degree and working as an actor in Toronto.

As noted in Chapter Two, May believes mothers have a significant impact on the next generation and, thus, on the world at large. In challenging patriarchal ideals of motherhood and of society in general, May practices matroreform by insisting on having open and honest relationships with her daughters and passing on her knowledge and experience of being a Black woman in a patriarchal and racist world. Having never been interested in supporting patriarchy, and always having wanted to make a difference in how her children are socialized, May paid close attention to how and what she taught them. For example, when they were young she read and provided her daughters with non-sexist books, watched and discussed TV and films with them, and enrolled them in workshops within the Black community that specifically dealt with racism and sexism, and in seminars and theatre groups that focused on ways to effectively understand and resist various forms of oppression.

May has always been especially conscious of her relationships with her daughters and well aware of the stories and teachings she passes on to them through her motherline. Not wanting to be domineering nor overpowering, she is self-reflexive about her interaction with her daughters and respects their ability to think and make their own decisions. She easily shares examples of her own mistakes and how she tries to learn from them, and also encourages her daughters to learn from, rather than repeat, her errors, as well as to be open to learning from their own missteps.[165] She invites them to discuss their ideas with her and respects and honours them when they openly challenge her attitudes, thinking, and behaviour:

> It's easy to lapse back to where your mother was and think in terms of male and female in the way you treat your children. I've always tried to talk to them a lot; even when I was going

> to Women's Studies I'd come home and share with the children what I'd been learning although they were little. I think they have a heightened sense of their own selves as women. Sometimes when I try to direct their lives they call me on it and I have to reflect and ask, "Why am I treating my daughter this way?" I'm always getting that check and it's good.

Because being feminist for May entails having control over her life and circumstances, being authentic, and trying not to limit herself and her opportunities because she is female, she has always encouraged her daughters "to be independent, to be free in their thinking, and to always question things like racism." Even though her daughters are now young adult women, May continues to speak with them about "how society is structured and how women become the way we are through being largely socialized by our role as mothers." Feminism for May entails "the liberation of women from all structures that have limited women in the past, and actively working towards restructuring society based on fair and equitable division of resources, including equal opportunity for women who are not to be treated differently from men because of the gender roles that society has proscribed."

When reflecting upon her experience of feminist mothering, May speaks highly of the values that her own mother who, while not a self-identified feminist, nevertheless modelled and passed along values by example that May identifies as feminist:

> I had a really good experience being a mother. I think my mother would never say she was a feminist, but I got a lot from her because when we were growing up my dad never wanted to give her money. She had to go and work to provide for us. She was a hard-working woman and she went out and worked her own farm and got our things and sent us to school. One of my sisters got married at 17 and my mom cried; she wanted us to get careers and learn how to take care of ourselves because she saw that in a married situation you don't have anything as a woman. So, she always encouraged us to go to school and get a job, take care of yourself,

> and then look for somebody. I found what she said was right. Without being able to provide for yourself, you will always be vulnerable to abuse, number one, and to falling into that trap of being a woman in this little box. So, it's the same thing I'm passing on and telling my kids.

In the spring of 2007, I had the honour of meeting and interviewing May's eldest daughter Gemma in Winnipeg just before she moved to Toronto where she would continue her career as a musician composing music, writing and singing lyrics, and producing popular music. On the cusp of her twenty-sixth birthday and recently divorced, Gemma self-identifies as biracial and feminist, noting "I've always felt that sometimes society views feminism as a negative thing, but I view it as a positive thing. I think it means that you believe women should be equal in all aspects of everything—in terms of getting paid the same, in terms of just being treated fairly. To me feminism's a positive thing."

During our conversation Gemma told me that she had always been aware of feminism, which she had learned from her mom and the activities that she was involved in: "She worked at the Immigrant Women's Association, and I think that she probably had conversations with us about it when we were younger. She always emphasized independence because a lot of women, I think, can grow up with having the idea of depending on someone, and depending on a man, she made that point indirectly. It was an idea that I kind of picked from her along the way."

Gemma credits her mother's feminism for her own sense of independence and the confidence she's developed and needs to work and succeed within the Canadian music industry: "I think that coming from the background I came from made it a lot easier for me to believe in myself as a musician; that I could do it and not think less of myself because I am a woman and not be intimidated by all the males that are there a lot of times telling you, 'I don't think so.' I think my mother encouraging us to be independent is a big part of that and knowing who we are."

As we talked Gemma continued to remember, with fondness and a chuckle in her voice, that May spent a lot of time with her and her younger sister when they were growing up, noting "She used to take us out everywhere. She spoiled us. We'd go out for dinners and have conversations about the world, and we'd have debates with each other and my mom would have us each take a side and write things down. We used to have a self-care basket in our house where it was 'pamper yourself and take time out for that too.'"

When I asked Gemma to reflect on how she understood her mother's feminism, she told me:

> I don't think it comes from a place of "I hate men" kind of thing. I don't think that's where my mom's coming from at all. I think it's about embracing yourself as a woman. And about overcoming those barriers set up for us as women that are just a part of society and those stereotypes. And finding the confidence to deal with it, and fight it in any way that you can [laugh]. I don't think it's a bad thing because I do think sexism is out there.

Gemma particularly mentions how May's background in journalism and her general tendency to ask a lot of questions has influenced her own propensity to "always question things, not in a suspicious way, but to see the whole picture and to pay attention to the underlying things that aren't said." Gemma also recognizes that her own feminist practice of asking questions informs her interactions with other women, and shares the following example from when she was a member of a girl pop group under contract with a Canadian record label: "I wanted to encourage the girls that our say was just as important as what the guys managing us in the business said. I feel as though we would have been treated differently had we been men. And so when we encountered those situations I would try and encourage them not to back down and to recognize the situation as being unjust. I lead by example."

During that time Gemma consciously paired up with another member of the popular music group, whose mother was a feminist and held similar feminist views, to model how they should be treated:

> We were both very headstrong, the two of us [giggle]. The rest of the group kind of had to follow along. And I think that we did get the point across that we weren't going to take it sitting down. There were a lot of times when I said, "If they were men they might not be treated like that." It goes so far in the music industry, especially because it's an industry where women can be viewed as sex objects a lot. And so it's just something else to be aware of and to make sure that you're always comfortable with everything that you're doing. And if you're not, speak up about it [laugh] because it's mostly men who are in the top positions in the industry. They definitely seem to be a lot quicker to doubt your skills when they know you're a woman. I think that because when it's all men there's an automatic comfort level there; they're more comfortable dealing with men. I think there's definitely more of a challenge for women. It just makes you have to push a little bit harder to make your voice heard.

Gemma acknowledges her close relationship with her mother, saying "We have a great relationship, me and my mom. She's such a great support and always there to offer advice and help with anything, and is someone I can talk to. I really value our relationship." Gemma also recognizes how May's solid teachings in good communication and self-confidence are directly linked to her mother's feminist understandings and practices of feminist parenting, to May's own mother's values, and to how she applies those lessons in her own professional life as a musician:

> I never really knew my mom's mom, my grandmother. But when I hear my mom talk about her I think that in her own way she kind of had some sort of feminist beliefs herself. I just remember her always—and this is something I think was passed down to my mom and she passed down to us—making sure that we were able to take care of ourselves. And I think it's a feminist kind of thing because in so many

> situations women can be left, if something happens in a marriage or something like that, to really struggle. I think it was something she passed down, the importance of independence. I wish I could have known her a bit more because she passed away. But I do think it's something that was passed down and then with my mom it became even [giggle] stronger. I know independence is something that you can pass down and it is something that you can teach your children. It's not even necessarily a conscious thing; it's just what you believe and basically skills for life that you need in order to survive.
>
> When it comes to working with a group of musicians, and it's usually all guys, I don't even think twice about it if I have to be directing and telling them what to do. It puts me in a place where I don't feel scared to do that, I feel confident. I think that I have their respect. I think having that confidence is where it all starts, and because I have it, it doesn't faze me to be delegating, whether it's in a group of men or women. It puts me in a position where I feel more confident coming from that background.

Gemma notes that as a girl she was unaware that her mom was consciously mothering her in a feminist way because it was just part of her upbringing. Yet, through our interviews Gemma recognizes that her mother was deliberately raising her daughters from a feminist perspective and that May's strategy of directly addressing discrimination based upon assumptions of gender, race, and ethnicity was effective. When envisioning the possibility of parenting her own daughter, Gemma declares, "I would want to prepare her for what's out there. And I'd want to instill a strong sense of self, which I think was at the root of everything my mom did when she was raising us. She wanted us to feel confident and not to be intimidated as a woman by anything that might come at us. It all starts with confidence and I would definitely talk about that with my daughter, if I ever have one."

Clearly the values and perspectives of Gemma's grandmother and mother have been passed on to her through May's feminist motherline. The development of Gemma's self-described independence and self-confidence, as well as her desire and skill to lead by example have come directly through the feminist teachings of, and relationship with, her mother. Gemma values and cherishes these attributes and is determined to pass them along to her own daughter, should she have one. She is also committed to passing along the critical skills of identifying, understanding, and contesting attitudes and acts of racism and sexism in her potential own feminist motherline.

Beverly, Sonia, and Kyla

At the time of our most recent interview in 2005, Beverly, age 57 years, defined herself as "an assimilated Ukrainian, single mother of two adult daughters who has always been critical of and contested traditional family structures." Having been partnered with another woman for the previous five years, she redefined her sexual orientation from bisexual to lesbian "primarily to give recognition to all those lesbians before me who had to struggle to come out as lesbian and what that means." Always concerned about social justice, she was working as a provincial project officer for the federal government developing programs addressing the victimization of women, girls, and queers.

Like other feminist mothers, Beverly has come to her understanding and critique of motherhood by reflecting upon her own circumstances and experiences of raising children, observing other women's experiences of mothering (including her own mother's), and talking with other mothers about their experiences of parenting. Beverly explained to me how historical structural shifts in familial organization from extended families to nuclear families and current myths associated with mothering contribute to the restrictions and damage women experience as mothers.[166] She believes many mothers living in Western developed nations experience isolation and low self-esteem because of the loss of the extended family and the emphasis on the nuclear family that requires mothers to be solely responsible for rearing their offspring.[167]

With the experience of raising young children as a mother in two different heterosexual nuclear families, and later as a single mother raising teenage daughters with limited support from their fathers, Beverly has firsthand knowledge of the isolating realities of mothering. She speculates that many mothers get to the point of not being able to cope because they experience isolation and lack substantial support within nuclear families, which often goes unnoticed due to the myth that women have a natural ability to mother and are expected to put the needs, wants, and desires of their husbands and children before their own.

Through her personal identity and creation of her own family, Beverly confronts the patriarchal model of the insular nuclear family being the only legitimate family form. She is well aware that her attitude, philosophy, and approach to mothering greatly differ from those prescribed by the institution of motherhood, noting "if your mothering comes from a place where you're constantly challenging conventional structures and notions then that's a political act in and of itself. And hopefully you're assisting your children to be able to critically analyze those same structures so that they can, in turn, challenge them where necessary and appropriate." Beverly's approach to matroreform is to provide a feminist motherline that offers a different model and discourse of how to be women and mothers than the one provided for her:

> One of the things that informed my mothering was the sense that women are strong in their own right, and we are capable of being independent and can critically analyze what's going on in the world around us. I was not big on women's roles; I did not want to mould my daughters into being like my mother, being a stay-at-home mom and that kind of thing. And so, I really pushed their education. I pushed for their sense of themselves to be able to be whatever they wanted to be.

Like May, Beverly models an alternative mothering practice for her children in her decision to parent alone and in her interpersonal relationships with her daughters. As a younger mother involved in feminist activist work she took her children to various meetings and events and engaged with them daily in ways that honoured their autonomy and individuality, acknowledging "I've had to treat my children in an equal fashion from the beginning so that they have always known that they have the right to express themselves, that they have the right to say 'No' and that we could engage in a dialogue about the issue as opposed to me wielding my power over them. And that's still very important to me."

When I met separately with Beverly's daughters, Sonia, age 31, and Kyla, age 28, over the same weekend in the fall of 2007, they had just returned to their respective homes in Toronto from a rare family vacation together with their mother overseas. Both daughters recognize how Beverly's feminist mothering has helped them develop into women with a strong sense of themselves and an understanding that mothering does not have to replicate the patriarchal model of motherhood. Their individual and collective experience as daughters of a feminist mother who contests the patriarchal script of motherhood and creates her own practice of parenting has instilled in them a belief that as autonomous women they, too, can choose to be mothers in their own way. Sonia and Kyla are both confident about, and openly welcome, the prospect of conceiving and parenting children in ways that trouble and counter conventional models of motherhood set by the institution of motherhood when they contemplate their further strategies of matroreform and feminist motherlines.

Beverly's elder daughter Sonia and I shared a tasty sushi dinner in a downtown Toronto restaurant. With a chuckle in her voice, the 31-year-old describes herself as a "yuppie—a young urban professional—working as an office manager for a law firm." In order to keep progressing up the ranks of her profession, she has taken a number of professional development courses related to negotiation, facilitation, and human resources since graduating with a diploma in facility management. At the time of our interview Sonia was exploring her eligibility for a master's program in disaster and emergency management.

When I asked Sonia if she identifies as a feminist she tells me she doesn't necessarily self-identify primarily as a feminist but does "embody most feminist values." She prefers to say that she's "a strong woman, as opposed to a feminist, because the word has become so loaded and very negative over the years." She was sure to tell me "I don't believe in the womyn with a 'y' perspective of feminism.'"[168] Sonia's experience of researching and reading the views of the conservative group REAL (Realistic, Equal, Active for Life) Women of Canada, and working on a project to develop a provincial women's health institute alongside "a lot of very, very strong women who identified as feminist" two years earlier, prompted her to identify as a feminist if directly asked. While she understands feminism to be "committed to working toward the same opportunities for men and women, and respecting the views of both genders equally," she describes her own feminism a bit differently:

> I'm actually not actively working to describe myself as a feminist; I'm not actively working to promote the cause, shall we say. I think that my best efforts are in being who I am and being good at what I do and when men get in my way, not backing down professionally. I really have a lot of guts and I go for it. Sometimes I think, "I don't know how I did that [laughs]. But I did!" And I realize, "I really don't care who you are. If I'm aware of these facts and I think that that's the right thing to do then I'm going to do that." It's not because I'm a feminist, it's because this is my job and this is who I am. And I'm not going to be womanly to accommodate what you think you should get out of this. I'm just going to be me [laughs].

Sonia understands that Beverly's feminism "involves a lot more of a fight" than her own does. She cites an example from her childhood of how her mom used to take her and Kyla, her younger sister, to the Take Back the Night marches and peace rallies to stand up for women's rights "not because it was about equality but because it was about women's rights." Sonia notes how the community aspect of Beverly's feminist activism was a large part of her life when Sonia and Kyla were young, and that making sure Beverly was "surrounded by people who were also working actively as *activists* in a certain box" was still important to her. Sonia compares her own connection with feminism to her association with religion, noting "I've never felt that I needed to become part of a particular community in order to have that certain strength within myself."

Continuing to reflect upon the distinction between their feminist perspectives, Sonia views Beverly's commitment to "fight for women's rights as being centred on women," whereas she sees her own "support for women's rights as an attempt to gain equality." Sonia wonders if the historical social context of women's struggles, which included much more of a fight for women's access to jobs, education, and political recognition during the 1970s and 1980s than in the mid 1990s and beyond, may influence and partially account for this difference in perspective. She also suggests that the decrease in the difficulty of middle-class women accessing well-paying jobs may also have a role to play in their differing approaches. For example, Sonia notes that her "heterosexual friends who are parents are discussing the costs and benefits of parental leave versus maternity leave when there isn't a primary wage earner or when the female partner makes more money than the male partner." Sonia suggests the fairly common situation of women earning equal or higher salaries than men within her circle of friends was an unlikely situation for women of her mother's generation.[169] She also recognizes that being the main wage earner changes the dynamic of romantic relationships and that she has a hard time accepting some feminist rhetoric that purports that she has "less opportunities because I'm a woman."

Reflecting on her childhood, Sonia admits with a giggle that she was "a bit of a strong-willed child and probably not the easiest child to parent." She credits her mother's feminism for her constant message that she and Kyla "could do anything and it didn't matter that you were a girl or a boy," and explains how she was supported by her mother equally when she pursued and studied fashion design and then engineering. Sonia believes being "dragged to and spending time at various marches and rallies as a youngster" gave her two perspectives about feminists and feminism when she was young. On the one hand she thought, "Oh, these women are crazy" because she didn't identify with the women or her mother at these events. On the other hand she thought, "What do you mean I can't do that because I'm a girl?" Anytime Sonia was faced with a decision that would perhaps have been gender identified in a certain way, she would think, "I'm doing it and I really don't care what you think" ([aughs]. Sonia recognizes there are many ways of being a feminist and provides an example of her mother —"a woman who works for the government with a complete pension, wears Birkenstocks with socks, and is in a relationship with another woman—and other women—who are in relationships with men, like to wear pretty strapless sundresses, and are writing their master's theses on women's issues"—as being on different points along a feminist spectrum.

Until fairly recently, Sonia and Beverly "knew each other very well" and had a "really excellent relationship that was very, very open." However, their relationship changed when Beverly started a romantic relationship with her current lesbian partner and made a conscious decision to no longer share everything with Sonia. Upon her own admission, Sonia "rebelled against the change which has lead to considerable tensions" between her and her mother. Yet, because Sonia has been raised to have a sense of agency and autonomy and to voice her opinion when she doesn't accept a situation, she never felt she "had to choke on [her] own feelings or suck it up."

Having recently ended a year-long relationship with a man fourteen years her senior because he wasn't interested in having (any more) children, Sonia is seriously considering having a child on her own. She directly credits her mother for this decision, noting "because my mother was a single mother for so long, and I know that she struggled with it but at the same time I don't think she did that badly, I figure I could probably manage okay somehow." Unafraid to have children alone, Sonia is prepared and planning to have a child on her own should she not find the partner she wants to be with. She plans, however, to ensure that she has a strong support network and notes how she and her friends from her university days have "formed a family unto [them]selves" and spend time together outside of [their] families of origin during holidays and the birthdays of each other and their children." Her closest friend and her husband, for example, have committed to being part of Sonia's support group should she become a single mother.

While Sonia would "like to be [her]self as a mother as opposed to some other version of what [her] mother is," she borrows heavily from her mother's feminist mothering practices when she remarks that she'd "try to make sure that [her] children's sense of self is strong." Sonia believes "feminist mothering is one of the most personal perspectives there is" and that "feminists will achieve their goals when their daughters don't care about it anymore because it's already a part of who they are." She anticipates working towards this goal in her own parenting by stressing her belief in equality for all humans, not solely for women.

Kyla, the younger of Beverly's two daughters, and I met over the lunch hour in Toronto that same weekend. She introduced herself as a 28-year-old bisexual, Jewish-Canadian woman who had ended a four-and-a-half year relationship with a woman in the past year and was going through an emotional transition.

Having completed her master's degree in urban planning two years earlier, she was currently employed by the Province of Ontario and working on affordable housing programs and related policy.

Kyla defines herself as feminist, and tells me "it's hard to be a feminist in my generation because there's not the same kind of community compared to my mother's generation when there was a present identity of being feminist." She believes she doesn't experience feminism in her everyday life to the same degree that her mother Beverly does, although she does try to be "actively present in certain situations." Kyla's understanding of feminism is informed by her mother's parenting, her formal high school and university education, her involvement in feminist activism as a university student, her year volunteering in a feminist organization in Israel, and her more recent experience of working in the public sector. Academically, Kyla understands feminism to be "a social movement that has been evolving since the first wave in the early 1900s." Professionally, Kyla draws upon her feminism when she deals with "some of the systemic discrimination that women face in the public sector," and particularly when she is "attempting to make the public sphere accessible and safe for the most disadvantaged in society, who are primarily women."

Like Sonia, Kyla respects Beverly's feminist mothering for instilling a sense of individual autonomy and agency to act for herself in her own life. By watching Beverly navigate her own relationship with members of her family of origin, which "was not necessarily the most progressive or feminist family," Kyla observed her mother try to be a different daughter than the one she was expected to be. She also observed how her mother tried to ensure "social cohesion" and "equity" in her family of creation and how she tried to remain "neutral" between her and Sonia by "making sure that everyone's voice [was] heard and refused to take sides because both were coming from equally good and sound places."

Kyla notes that she struggled as a child with her mother's "central values and teachings in her child rearing," and claims she needed a lot of attention as a young child and speculates that she desired a lot of attachment to and validation from her mom. When she was very upset about something as a child, Kyla would have self-described temper tantrums. Part of Beverly's strategy of dealing with these situations was to tell Kyla when she was in the midst of a meltdown, "you're going to have to find a way to deal with this," and then briefly leave the house for a short walk. Beverly always returned and talked in a very supportive way with Kyla once she had cooled down. As a teen, Kyla remembers her mom "wouldn't pry into [her daughters'] personal lives," but would rather have them "try and figure out the situation for [themselves] and figure out how [they] could find whatever strengths [they] had to cope with it." Kyla often wished her mom would simply provide the answer she was seeking.

Due to the many open discussions Beverly and her daughters had about women and their roles within society, Kyla believes her mother "instilled a foundational value of being able to understand the world as patriarchal" and, as a result, the girls "didn't have to struggle to uncover or figure it out alone." While Kyla pursued feminist studies in university and has come to her own understanding of gender, patriarchy, and how the world functions, she credits her mother for engaging her in discussions about women in different facets of life. She notes that as adults, they "don't really talk about feminism because in a lot of ways we probably share pretty common perspectives on how we understand it."

Kyla thinks that many women of her "generation accept the more mainstream advances that feminism has provided for them within the workplace and the home, and believe that nothing else needs to done." She speculates that within her contemporaries "there's even a kind of perspective that we don't need to apply a feminist analysis because women are in management or women aren't just mothers who stay at home." As a professional, Kyla has not found a community of like-aged feminists, although she notes older women within the profession continue to be actively engaged in feminist work. She also wonders what it means for her "generation that doesn't have to face some of the struggles [her] mother's generation had to face because [her] generation is much more comfortable with having more fluid and multiple identities and is able to carry more because [they] haven't had to struggle that much as feminist or as bisexual women." Reflecting on her own identity, she claims "I get to hold both of those and, as a Jewish woman, I have all of these multiple identities and I want to figure them all out because there's not just one."

Kyla is well aware of the ways in which her mother breaks traditional family roles and conventional models of motherhood, not only in choosing to parent differently from the ways of her own mother, but also in the feminist values Beverly embodies and enacts in her parenting. Kyla also believes alternative ways of creating family and parenting are a viable option for her. While in her previous lesbian relationship, Kyla and her partner seriously considered starting a family together. When thinking about the possibility of being a mother, Kyla asserts:

> I absolutely think there would be a role for feminism to play in how I might parent a child. Although I don't yet know, entirely, what that role is. I think that there has been more and more anecdotal research and magazine articles that put more emphasis on nature in terms of our genetic makeup and gender identities that I understand can be quite fluid. However, there is more to male and female and these two dichotomies may come from this genetic place and that would probably become more of my struggle; how do I have a little baby and not try to decide what kind of gender identity they have, while at the same time see what they are bringing out themselves and respecting that and them?

Kyla takes the work of parenting seriously; "it's political in and of itself to take a political perspective and decide to parent in a feminist way. It's also political in the sense that you have so much impact on your children in terms of who they become and how they are in the world. Who they are is going to have a great impact [laugh]."

Both Sonia and Kyla, like Gemma, are well aware of the ways in which their mother, Beverly, has chosen to intentionally parent in ways that honour her own feminism. They recognize that their mother took risks and struggled to ensure that she was able to practice her vision of matroreform. And like Gemma, they are also able to identify their mother's feminism as being the foundation of their own identities and abilities as strong and independent women. The desire to mother children in the future in ways that counter the patriarchal discourse and practice of institutional motherhood are well within their imaginations and plans. Furthermore, they are not fearful of parenting in ways that suit their particular circumstances and, in the case of Sonia, have begun to think about and make arrangements to ensure that they will be supported if and when the time comes. They are purposely planning to continue engaging in their mothers' feminist motherline, as well as continue and develop their own practices of matroreform.

Paula and Meagan

Born in 1956 in England to a father of Colombian ancestry and a mother of Australian heritage, Paula and her younger sister were raised in Canada by their single mother. When we first met in the mid 1990s, Paula was in her mid 40s and in the process of leaving her common-law male partner and father of their three children, then age 11, eight, and four years. When we meet more recently in July of 2005, she was on the cusp of celebrating her 49th birthday and feeling a little "empty-nested" because her children, now teenagers and older, were more independent and, therefore, no longer needing her to "think about or take responsibility" for them as much. With her two younger children, a daughter age 13, and a son age 17, living with their father every other week and her eldest daughter, age 20, spending plenty of time away from home, Paula was experiencing a lot more personal time than she had for many years. The regular monthly child support cheques from the children's father meant she was able to expand her massage therapy business into a successful storefront practice and to provide a more stable, although still quite low, income for herself and her children.

Paula had recently become certified in conflict resolution, specializing in organizational leadership. Although the course took her three years to complete due to the long-term effects of a serious chemical injury she suffered on the job in her 20s, she found the training helpful to her personal life and in assisting her friends deal with various problems. Since Paula is very sensitive to perfumes and chemicals, particularly herbicides and insecticides, she periodically spends time in Kenora and Thunder Bay, Ontario, to avoid and cleanse herself of the pesticides from the annual mosquito fogging and public use of herbicides in Winnipeg.

Over the past number of years Paula has become more open to and has been learning more about her South American indigenous roots through her infrequent contact with her aging father who telephones her approximately "once a year for a two- to three-minute controlled conversation." Through this experience she has "developed more compassion for his reality and a better understanding of the political environment that influenced his life, the degree of cruelty that existed in his family since the time of the conquistadores, and how that travels down through the generations." She has also found a way to bring her understanding of the historical and current violence in Colombia into her massage practice, having joined together with others to pursue funding to provide massage therapy for immigrant and refugee survivors who have been subjected to state-sanctioned torture in their home countries, and to potentially assist those who have survived police abuse and residential schools in Canada.

As a young woman, Paula was not drawn to the term "feminist" because she was first introduced to it "in a man-hating context," which conflicted with her experience of "less competition dealing with boys than with girls." However, she soon incorporated being feminist as part of her identity when she entered the labour force and witnessed males having easier access to jobs and being taken more seriously than females. Since becoming a mother in her late 20s and early 30s, Paula's feminism has "transformed from being a reaction to oppression to an act of making a contribution to nurturing and building a new culture of growing and giving."

Because she believes public action is a way to teach children about their connection to the community and the importance of being socially responsible, Paula and her partner would take their young children to various demonstrations in Winnipeg. As a family they attended rallies during the Gulf War and the siege at Kanehsatà:ke, slept in the Peace Village on the Manitoba Legislature grounds, engaged with Building Peace Through Play and participated in Take Back the Night marches. Paula considers these actions "important family social and community-building events because it is important to show kids to put your body where your ideas are."

At the time of our 2005 interview, Paula and her three children were living in Winnipeg in a women's housing co-op that had a female head of household policy that supported families headed by single lesbian and heterosexual women, lesbian couples, and the occasional heterosexual couple. Paula credits this experience for her youngest daughter's "interest in women's rights and the history of women's rights, and in her pride that women are running the building she lives in." Because "living in the Co-Op also normalizes lesbian relationships, and other non-heterosexual unions," her children also "see how various ways of being a family are possible."

Living together in a small space has meant that Paula and her children "have bonded and practice a lot of honesty, openness, and sharing." Growing up as the "eldest in a single-parent family who did too much surrogate parenting," Paula "never wanted any of [her] children to have to take on the responsibility of child rearing and domestic labour and intentionally did not put those responsibilities on [her] children in any practical terms." She confesses she "might even have gone overboard" because she finds it difficult to get her children to carry their fair share of domestic work. In talking about her eldest daughter, Meagan, she asserts, "In fact, she used to argue that if I would ask her to do the dishes I was trying to put her in a female ghetto" [laughter].

While Paula thinks "feminism has to include everyone because we're all on a continuum," she also believes that "only each individual can determine their role within it." She argues that "social interactions and institutions within our society need to change" if we are to ensure equality for all people. Feminism, for Paula, means recognizing the need for change and taking whatever action she can to make those changes: "Being feminist means being political, it inspires both inward actions—how I run my life—and outward actions—how I raise my children and attend public demonstrations."

When Meagan and I met in the spring of 2007, she described herself as a 22-year-old indigenous, South American and Euro-Canadian woman, and the eldest daughter of "dedicated and intentional parents." Also self-identifying as feminist, she thought that "everyone should be a feminist," while also admitting to "only occasionally identifying as feminist in public." Conscious of her decision, she confessed, "In some ways it feels really sneaky and awful [laugh] to pick and choose how often I use the word feminist but I think it scares a lot of people off. And people have lots of preconceived notions of what those values are and occasionally would think I want to offend them. They might be able to identify a little bit more easily with where I'm coming from if I don't use the term to identify myself." For Meagan feminism is:

> about making space for people to treat one another well, to treat themselves well, to treat other beings well, and to live well. I'm a feminist because I think if we can take care of one another then we're going to be able to create a better world for ourselves and for other beings too. I believe it's important to include everyone in decision making, in growth, in change, and in healthy living. Right now there is not peace and harmony among cell populations which is due in large part, in my opinion, to the patriarchy that we live with.

From Meagan's perspective, "people aren't naturally predisposed to being submissive, to being oppressed, or to having someone else make decisions for them." Rather, she continues to explain, this behaviour "comes from learning to be in that position or being taught that it's important to be in that position, which, in part, comes from the ideas perpetuated in religious and mythical ideas and cultural attitudes that claim it's okay for part of the population to have more power than another that are in our culture."

Feminism has been part of Meagan's value system for as long as she can remember and recalls a specific incident as a 10-year-old living in a small conservative town outside of Winnipeg to explain. Meagan knew it wasn't fair when she and her girlfriend were prevented from playing soccer with the boys at recess. Although the boys were told by the teachers that they weren't allowed to say no to the girls who wanted to play, the teachers didn't tell the boys that they had to let the girls play often or treat them nicely. Meagan recalls another example as a teenager when she was "asked out on dates by older men" and quickly learned about sexual exploitation by the way the men would respond, either by backing away or continuing to pursue a sexual relationship with her, when they found out her young age. She relays the current importance of her feminism in a more recent experience of observing sexist attitudes expressed by a close friend and how this has made her realize that dating someone who is feminist is very important to her.

Meagan credits her identity as a feminist primarily to her mother, as well as to her father and to the communities they raised her with and through. She cites, in particular, "the feminists who talked a lot about feminism and wanted everyone to feel the same, and the people who left their church because women weren't allowed a greater role." She is particularly grateful that both of her parents honestly explained "how babies are made" when she asked them as a very young child and believes this approach "is a huge step in raising children in a way that is honest and allows them to be aware of what sexuality is about, and opens the door to allow children to learn more about their own bodies later." Her parents' feminist values also included teaching her how to think for herself which, she admits, drove her "crazy" at times because they'd always ask her "'Well, what do you think?' or 'What would you do?' when [she] just wanted them to tell [her] how to spell the word or how to do something." Her folks were very cautious about the kind of toys Meagan and her siblings were given as gifts and were allowed to play with. They were also careful about the kind of media their children were exposed to. Meagan fondly recalls falling asleep as her parents watched the *CBC* TV news and how they would always talk with her about the often horrific news stories featured.

While reluctant to define anyone else's politics, Meagan believes her mother's feminism is quite similar to her own, noting "it's not limited to just white female academics and politics, but encompasses everybody, including men and children because everyone benefits from a feminist society and community." Meagan perceives a difference in their "views around patriarchy," noting "mom has a more cynical view about how the outside world has affected people in her community because she has seen people close to her do stuff that she really thinks is awful or hurtful, whereas I have a lot less patience and faith in how things are being run by the powers that be and have more faith in the grassroots community work and the people around me, and in people changing their minds and behaviours."

While Meagan's ideas about feminism first developed by observing her mother, they have continued to grow as she applies her own understandings of feminism to her life:

> I'm always trying to find work that I will feel ethical about in terms of where the money is coming from, what the work is about, who I'm with, and how I make other people feel when I do it. Like providing child care for friends of mine, which is the kind of work I want to do. I'm all about the human experience and it's also what I'm studying through acting. It's really crucial to me to be able to honour the human spirit. I think our society has forgotten, in our rush for power and following our patriarchal structures, some of the more visceral experiences we need as humans to stay healthy—emotionally, mentally, and spiritually.

At the time of our interview, Meagan was in a relationship with another feminist woman and shared her thoughts about how feminism is integral to her life, particularly when reflecting on potentially becoming a mother:

> Feminism starts, not only in the decision-making process to raise children, but, also in that process of deciding if it's something that I want to do, or that I and a potential partner might want to do together. If that was the case, it would also involve setting things up for that child; how is this child going to come into my/our life?
>
> I think deciding on the HOW is really important. Is it an adoption choice? Is it a biological choice? Is it a surrogate mother choice? Like, all of those different possibilities, and there are many of them. If it's biological, whose sperm is it? Whose womb is it?
>
> All of those things are really intertwined with feminism. Not only because those questions are going to be asked by the child, but also because it affects the relationship with the child too, and how they're going to view themselves. So I think that's really important.

> I don't really believe your personal politics can be separated from how you live your life. I find it very contrary if they are separated. Raising children is a political act.

Clearly Meagan has been influenced by her mother's feminist parenting and feminist motherline. According to Meagan, her feminism is "pretty much the same" as her mother's. Like her mother Paula, Meagan also understands feminist mothering to be a conscious political act of disturbing conventional ideals of mothering, motherhood, and parenting. Meagan's awareness of the ways in which her feminism informs her daily interactions with friends and strangers, and how and when she chooses to use the term "feminist" in those interactions attests to the prevalence of her feminist upbringing and the perseverance to her mother's feminist motherline. Meagan's decisions about the kind of paid and voluntary labour she takes on, the kinds of working and personal relationships she engages in, and her thinking around her potential role and responsibilities of parenting speak to her understanding and respect for matroreform and the value of feminist motherlines.

Shar and Darcy

In the late spring and early summer of 2007, I had the very good fortune of spending time with both Shar, almost 62 years and the only grandmother in the group of feminist mothers I spoke with, and her eldest daughter Darcy, then age 39. Together they talked about their understandings of feminism, mothering, the interconnection of the two, and how feminist mothering influences their lives. Shar told us that her feminism is "not merely a theory but rather an embodied political worldview that informs [her] entire life." She thinks that "feminism, like mothering, needs to ideally be a lifetime commitment" and that "You can't just kick the kid out when he's 18 and think you're finished mothering. You can't read a few books and say, 'I'm a feminist, now I'm done.' I won't be finished mothering or feministing [laughter] until I die." Clearly, feminism and mothering are strongly connected for Shar, and she believes, as noted in Chapter Two, that feminist mothering is a conscious feminist political act that has political implications.

Being aware that all interactions are significant and have far-reaching effects in the lives of people and on society in general, Shar attempts to make deep and real connections with children rather than follow what she perceives to be conventional practices of "consistently lying to children, telling them to be quiet and ignoring their needs."

Children have been part of Shar's life for over five decades. Her earliest memories are as the only sister to three brothers growing up in an abusive family where her alcoholic father verbally, emotionally, and physically abused everyone around him, particularly his sons. As a 10-year-old she remembers having a strong sense that if her parents would give her money and leave her alone she could do a better job of raising her brothers than they were doing.

Not wanting to replicate her own childhood, Shar chose to marry a long-time boyfriend who she describes as "supportive, gentle and kind" because he was unlike the men she had grown up around. At the age of 23 and early in her marriage Shar began her family. She first birthed a daughter and then a son three years later, and three years after that adopted a second daughter. She recalls being "fairly controlling about decisions and practices" related to her children and their upbringing; she wanted everything done in a certain way and had a husband who accommodated her wishes. When her 12-year marriage ended, Shar became solely responsible for their three children because her relationship with her former husband had become "estranged." She attended university, earned a teaching degree, and subsequently briefly taught children in the public school system. In 2007 Shar was running a child-care centre out of her home and was spending as much time as she could with her recently adopted pre-school aged daughter and her two pre-teenaged grandchildren.

As a single mother, Shar held a number of part-time teaching positions in the public school system, taught public speaking, was active in several feminist organizations, and often appeared in local newspapers and on television for her political activism around abortion, anti-pornography, violence against women, and women in advertising. Shar believes she was unable to secure a full-time teaching position because of her reputation as an active and outspoken feminist. Since she was overtly political in her personal and public life, her first three children grew up listening to her ideas, overhearing her speak on the phone, and going with her to many feminist meetings, marches, and rallies.

As a new mother, Shar had a "gut awareness" that she has since developed. Having always abhorred violence, she always tries to create a non-violent environment and home for herself and for her children. She has never found it necessary to hit or overpower her children, has never allowed violent toys around her children or in her home, and continues to prevent violent interaction between people, including teasing and sarcastic humour which she thinks is "vicious." Shar consciously treats her own children and the children in her child care with love, gentleness, flexibility, and playfulness. Discipline has never been an issue for Shar because she quickly learned as a young mother that the more she responded and trusted her children's sense of what they needed, the less frustration and aggression they experienced and expressed. Working through problems by talking and listening both resolves problems and teaches children that they are loved and how to take responsibility for their decisions and for themselves. Shar notes that she continues to practice the lessons and approaches she first developed raising her own children when caring for the children in her daycare:

> My daycare children are absolutely aware that they are loved. That's something that I'm able to hold right there all the time. Listening to them is consistent. Even when I'm at my worst moment in the daycare, the child speaks and I hear what they say. And if I don't have time to answer them immediately, I'll

> say, "[child's name], I heard what you said. Can you wait just a second? 'Cause right now I'm doing this other thing and I can't really pay attention. But, I know, I heard you and I will pay attention in just a minute."
>
> I'm trying to acknowledge that they are real. So much of what goes on in the culture is a denial of the reality of their being. It's wanting to pretend they're not really there, so we don't have to acknowledge their life.
>
> One of the kids came to the daycare very upset. One of the other kids was going to her daycare and she would talk about the fact that kids were being hit at daycare. And I looked at him and said, "[child's name], I would never hit you because I love you. If anybody hits you, they don't love you." And I said, "I would never say to you that I love you and then some other time I would hit you." And he said, "I know."

As we sat together with Shar in Darcy's home that summer evening in 2007, Darcy identified herself as a Euro-Canadian mother of a 12-year-old daughter and seven-year-old son, and a feminist who is very close to her feminist mother. Although she was still adjusting to her new identity as a divorced woman, Darcy was finding it relatively easy being a single mother, in part, because her husband often travelled as part of his job and she'd been responsible for and doing most of the parenting alone during her marriage. The fact that both of their children attend Shar's home-run child care, that her daughter spends one night a week with her grandmother, and that she and her mother and their families generally spend "a ton of time together" are also helpful. Having a BA, in addition to several college early childhood courses, and several years of experience working as an Educational Assistant working with children in a specialized reading program at an inner city school in Winnipeg also give Darcy some of the skills she has found useful to mothering.

While Darcy identifies herself as feminist, she points out that she's not a "radical active feminist who's vigorously involved in politics, protests, and current issues." Rather, she defines her feminism as "an underlying philosophy that can rear its head at times, and not at others, that's based on rights for women, and respects the work that other women have done to allow [her] and others to be where we are today." Darcy thinks that because many young women and women in her peer group don't know about the history of their feminist foremothers they are either unaware of the opportunities open to them or take those opportunities for granted. Darcy feels frustrated when she appears to be the only person who notices and speaks up about what she considers "obvious gender inequality." She recalls, for example, having to address the sexist depiction of stereotypical gender career opportunities on various posters at the school where she works. She confides that she finds the sexist and sexualizing lyrics of popular music and the gendered advertising for clothes and toys difficult to tolerate because "gender inequality brings on a vicious streak [in her] when it's related to parenting."

Darcy calls herself a "mother snob" and believes that she has been greatly influenced by her mother's feminist approach to, and example of, caring for her and her siblings, for her own children, and for the children in her mom's home-based child care. Darcy's own experiences of working in various daycare centres and within the school system have also informed her attitude and approach to mothering. Continuing Shar's feminist mothering practice of critically analyzing popular culture, especially television programs and advertisements, means that Darcy is critical of the ways in which toys and clothing are stereotypically gendered, particularly how they (hetero)sexualize girls and encourage aggressive and violent behaviour in boys. Lately she has been horrified by the slogans and narrative she has read on some of the T-shirts worn by children in the elementary school where she works. She tells me about two worn by elementary school-age girls that she finds particularly offensive, "Hold my purse while I kiss your boyfriend" and "I'm not fat, I'm big boned."

Like her mother, Darcy attempts to interact with her children in ways that provide space for them to develop as complex, individual whole people who know they are loved and have a healthy sense of self-esteem. And like Shar, who has always been very critical of media and its message, Darcy teaches her children to be aware of the packaging of toys and the often gendered and sexualized advertising that accompanies it. She and her children watch TV and movies together, often skipping or zipping through TV ads on recorded programs or vacating the room during commercial breaks. Keenly aware of the pressure of advertising on children, not only to buy certain products, toys, and brands, but also to take on stereotypical gender roles and sexist attitudes, Darcy doesn't allow her children to wear clothing with words on them. She is also vigilant about screening, talking about, and analyzing the force and messages of advertising with her children:

> We stay out of what we call the "pink zone" at Toy R Us. You know the "Barbie, dress-up princess isle." On the other side of it, we stay out of the "flaming truck, boy, violent knife aisle." I don't like those aisles because I want my daughter to be a powerful person. I don't want her to be a princess rescued, and I don't want my son to be a violent person. I want them to use all parts of themselves, their brains and their bodies. I don't want them to be limited by a toy choice or commercial they've seen on TV. I want it to be open for my kids. I want them to be able to do whatever it is that they want to do.

As a girl and young woman, Darcy recognized that Shar was unlike any of the her friends' mothers; "she was feminist, outspoken and, didn't shave her body hair or wear a bra." Darcy's friends enjoyed hanging out at her house and spent many hours talking with Shar, just as Darcy and her siblings did. Darcy and Shar have always been very close and over time their bond has grown closer with the birth of Darcy's children and more recently with the adoption of Shar's daughter and Darcy's youngest sister. Given that Darcy's husband travelled a fair amount with his job, she and Shar spent a lot of time together. When her babies arrived, Darcy depended on Shar, who happily slept on the floor next to the beds of her grandchildren for the first six weeks of their lives. Since the adoption of Shar's youngest child, Darcy and Shar have switched roles in some ways, with Darcy advising Shar on matters related to infants and young babies.

The two mothers share a very intimate relationship, and together they demonstrate how they often finish each other's sentences and how they only say little fragments of sentences because they'll know what the other one's talking about in two or three words. They also constantly discuss their beliefs about the ways in which they raise their children and the thought they put into their motherwork, particularly around values, communication, and the types of toys, books, movies, and clothes they should encourage and allow.

Darcy acknowledges the ways in which she has been influenced by her mother's feminism, which she respects and models for herself and her children. For instance, she believes reproductive choice needs to be available for all women who need to make that decision, although she cannot ever imagine having an abortion herself. She credits her public speaking ability and media awareness to her mother, noting, "I'm pretty much spewing exactly what she said to me." Darcy asserts that their values around and strong stance on non-violent play and fundamental belief that all people need to be loved and learn how to care for themselves and others are almost identical. Both mothers also think it's absurd that society expects men to know how to care for children. Darcy says: "We don't give dolls to boys; how do we then hand them a new baby and expect them to father? We train girls their entire lives, why aren't we doing it with boys?"

Shar understands that her position and role of mother and grandmother is unique and special, reflecting, "I've had the privilege most grandparents don't have in having a huge hand in raising my grandchildren as well as being a pseudo parent in some ways. Not many grandmothers adopt a child that is not their grandchild." She describes her co-parenting relationship and practice with Darcy as very intimate:

> I end up in this situation where I'm saying to my daughter, "This is what I want for my grandchildren" and she's saying, as the mother of those children, "This is what I'd rather you say." We have situations where the kids don't want to go home with her and they want to stay at day care or want to stay at grandma's house rather than go home. We have to decide what we're going to do and sometimes we figure out a way for them to stay with me.

Self-respect and effective and respectful communication, which have always been important to Shar, are also are important to Darcy, to their relationship with each other and to the relationships they have with children. Honesty and respect are values that these two mothers honour and try to practice. In the past five years or so, Shar has begun to extend these values beyond her family of creation and the relationships with the children in her child care by beginning to reconcile some of the differences and hard feelings between herself and her brothers, her parents, and her former husband.

Darcy continues her mother's practice of matroreform and feminist motherline by consciously collaborating with Shar to deliberately challenge the institution of motherhood, and to negotiate the social and cultural obstacles to the self-determination and agency of their children and of themselves as women and mothers. Individually and collaboratively they chip away at and challenge the insistence of gender socialization that limits nurturing to only girls and women and values aggression and violence in boys and men. They offer different values and practices to their children and to the children that they engage with during their paid work. As self-described co-parents, they spend time together talking about and consciously raising their respective children, and Darcy's youngest sister and Shar's grandchildren in ways that do not replicate, but rather trouble and contest patriarchal ideals of motherhood and parenting. In doing so, they both continue, as other feminist mothers do, to challenge patriarchal social motherhood norms and raise their children to be autonomous people, who have the skills to think critically about gender relations and the world they live in.

Feminist Mothers and Their Feminist Daughters Creating Feminist Motherlines

The above reflections of the five daughters of four feminist mothers offer concrete examples of the existence of matroreform and feminist motherlines and the explicit ways in which their mothers' practice of matroreform and feminist motherlines are understood and acknowledged. Clearly each mother/daughter duo has created their own interpersonal dynamic and unique way in which they create and practice their feminist motherline. Each mother and each daughter have a distinctive understanding of feminism, yet also share similar perspectives on some issues. They all appreciate and respect their differences and honour the ways in which their feminism overlaps.

Elements of the survival and continuation of each of the feminist motherlines can be heard in the voices of the daughters as they reflect upon the feminist lessons their mothers have taught them, the ways in which they interpret their mothers' feminism, the ways in which their own feminism is similar to and/or differs from their mothers, and the ways in which their mothers' feminist values and mothering practices will most likely be an element of their own mothering practices, whether they are held, carried forward, and/or challenged.

Each of the five feminist daughters speaks of how she, as a child of a feminist mother, has learned to be an autonomous and independent woman and suggests that there is a strong probability that she will continue the practices of matroreform and feminist motherlines should she become a parent. Individually and collectively they all honour their mother's feminist parenting and motherlines, recognize how they have benefited from it, and that it does, or likely will, inform their own practice of feminist mothering.

CONCLUSION

Practicing Feminist Mothering

Feminist mothering is a living thing.[170]

My hope in writing *Practicing Feminist Mothering* has been to respond positively to the call, first made by second wave feminists and subsequently sustained by third wave feminists, to critique patriarchal constructs and narratives of motherhood as outlined in my overview of the history of feminism and motherhood in Chapter One, and to also reveal and understand the practical complexities of motherhood and mothering for women. By continuing the feminist commitment and practice of placing women's knowledge and experiences at the centre of inquiry that is so essential to feminist research and theorizing, I have drawn upon the experiences and knowledge/s of a small group of self-identified feminist mothers, and some of their daughters, living in a particular geographical region during a specific historical period. My focus has been to attend to the ongoing need to explore the realities of feminist mothering.

In this final chapter I offer a concise overview of the realities of feminist mothering as described by feminist mothers and their daughters in Chapters Two, Three and Four, which, as noted in Chapter One, has been lacking in previous scholarship on motherhood and mothering. I also introduce and explain three main overarching themes that I have identified in the parenting practices of these families which have resulted from the particular ways in which they parent. I conclude by raising some questions and suggestions for feminism and the field of maternal scholarship to consider.

The Realities of Feminist Mothering

Feminism

Through the generosity of their time and their commitment to honouring and developing feminist knowledge, theory, and herstory, these mothers and daughters have each patiently explained how they make sense of feminism. As detailed in Chapter Two, the original group of mothers experience feminism as an embodied worldview that acknowledges and critiques patriarchy, is critical of the construction, hierarchy, and power dynamics of gender, and also understands that the personal experiences of people are linked with and influence the social and political contexts within which they live. Their feminism values individual autonomy and choice, which are essential to human self-determination and social change, and encompasses the conscious act of putting their theoretical and experiential knowledge of feminism into practice in their daily lives, particularly in their mothering.

Feminism for the daughters, as discussed in Chapter Four, has been variously influenced by their mothers' parenting and, as a result, is unsurprisingly similar to that of their mothers. Unlike the general trend of matricide in American feminism over the ages, as addressed by Susan Faludi in an article in *Harper's Magazine* October 2010, the daughters of these feminist mothers are not interested in killing off their mothers, nor their mothers' feminism.[171] Rather, their feminism, much like that of their mothers, is part of their identity and their value system that recognizes and is critical of patriarchy and the politics of gender in all elements of life. They also value human autonomy and independence, particularly for women and children, and are aware of the constraints placed on women as mothers within the narrowly constituted and idealized institution of motherhood, as theorized by feminists such as Jessie Bernard, Betty Friedan, Sharon Hays, Andrea O'Reilly, and Adrienne Rich. All these daughters believe that feminism does or will inform their motherwork and their relationships with their (potential) children, and confirms the existence of, and commitment to, the matroreform and feminist motherlines that their mothers have created, developed, and continue to engage in.

Matroreform

Thanks to these forthright women, we are able to better understand the ways in which their feminism informs their understanding and practices of mothering, as well as the complicated realities and complexities of mothering and motherhood, as explained in Chapter Three. Feminist mothers and daughters understand, and are critical of, the pressure and cost of conforming to a patriarchal model of motherhood and the real consequences of non-compliance. They also believe there is room for resistance, intervention, and renewal within its structure. Rather than acquiesce to the expectations associated with the institution of motherhood, or reject motherhood completely as some did during the second wave of feminism, these feminist mothers reform their parenting by actively resisting elements of its confining configuration and create different ways of mothering, as noted in Chapters Two and Three.

This practice of matroreform entails the difficult and often complicated work of parenting from a place of empowerment that is critical of and defies patriarchal ideals and expectations by breaking its rules and replacing them with alternative approaches to mothering. The authority and agency to do so are directly related to the mothers' feminist consciousness and to their belief and confidence in their ability and right to reform motherhood by (re)defining and (re)structuring mothering for themselves and for their children. These feminists differ from those who felt silenced during the 1970s and 1980s due to their capacity to draw upon their own knowledge and experience of feminism and mothering that they understand to be valuable and valid.

They are also aware of and consciously contest the oppressive patriarchal institution of motherhood by inventing and practicing a counter-practice of mothering to the harmful one prescribed. Unlike some of the feminist theorists and feminist mothers noted in Chapter One, such as Robin Morgan and Marianne Hirsch, who were unable to take on the sisterhood mantle of second wave feminism without throwing mothering out with the bathwater because they felt criticized for being mothers, these feminist mothers have chosen to be vocal—rather than silent—about their mothering and motherwork within feminist circles. While not always supported or understood by their feminist sisters, they nevertheless speak of their realities and actively (re)constitute mothering for themselves and engage in relationships with their children that refuse to replicate the structures, narratives, or lessons of patriarchal hierarchy within the mother/child relationship.

In fact, these feminist mothers appear to have responded to Marianne Hirsch's call for a "mother inclusive feminism" that recognizes the infinite differences among mothers and the vast complexity of mothering experiences and knowledge while concurrently resisting the idealization of motherhood. Rather than essentialize their experiences in relation to their mothering, as some feminists have done in the past, these feminist mothers envision and engage in meaningful feminist practice both within and outside of motherhood with the goal to make significant lasting social change.

Motherlines

Implicit in the mothering of these feminists is the practice of constructing and maintaining feminist motherlines to ensure that their feminist motherwork is visible, and potentially carried on by their children into the future. They, like feminists before them, understand that motherlines extend back to their own mothers and forward to the next generation, in this case to and through their daughters. By attending to and sharing their maternal practices and linking them to reflections and understandings of their own relationships with their own mothers/parents as daughters, they actively work to forge strong bonds with their children and to create new feminist mothering practices that both counter and reform those of mainstream motherhood.

The effects of creating a feminist motherline include the continuity of feminist ideals and the importance of gender analysis in both generations, and the continuation of similar attitudes, philosophies, and approaches to mothering which promise to sustain and inform, as noted by both mothers and daughters in Chapter Four, the persistence of feminist praxis in both generations over time.

Perhaps this generation of feminist mothers has been better able to actively model and speak to their children about their feminist mothering than earlier generations of feminists because they have been able to more fully integrate their feminism with their mothering. This shift likely came about from the theoretical work of Jessie Bernard and Adrienne Rich and the more recent theorizing of Sharon Hays and Andrea O'Reilly who all address the distinction between motherhood and mothering and the role of patriarchy in repressing women within the role of mothering. Understanding that patriarchal motherhood, and not mothering, is restrictive and repressive for women has allowed for more empowered mothering practices that are open and engaged with children.

The evidence of feminist motherlines can be seen in the comments of daughters who confirm that feminist motherlines have taught them the critical skills necessary to observe, understand and contest the culture of patriarchy, and more specifically the maternal and motherhood expectations placed on women. For instance Darcy, the daughter of Shar, who is raising her own children, notes the ways her mothering is informed by her feminism as well as by her mother's feminist mothering practices, while those daughters not yet mothers reflect upon how they may consider to parent should they become mothers. Unlike some feminists during the early second wave who were unable to speak openly about their experiences as mothers and therefore did not actively engage in or promote motherlines, these mothers are consciously aware of and speak about their feminist motherlines as explicit counter-narratives to patriarchal mothering and motherhood, which may be implemented by their daughters.

Themes Evident in *Practicing Feminist Mothering*

Having reviewed the general realities of feminist mothering as described by feminist mothers and their daughters, I now turn to three additional overriding themes that have emerged from my conversations about feminist mothering with feminist mothers and their daughters: Feminist mothering is a conscious political act, the practice of feminist mothering is messy, and the practice of feminist mothering is a living entity that simultaneously values change and continuity.

Feminist Mothering is a Political Act

One obvious theme within *Practicing Feminist Mothering* is that feminist mothering is a deliberate and purposeful political act. While this is undoubtedly claimed and acknowledged in Chapters Two and Four by both feminist mothers and daughters because of their deliberate incorporation of feminism into their everyday lives, it is also seen as the foundation of feminist parenting through the conscious use of the term "feminist mother" in the mothers' self-definitions and identities. It is also evident in Chapter Three when the mothers explain how they are explicitly enacting matroreform as a counter-narrative to patriarchal motherhood.

By separating the possibility of autonomous, mother-centred parenting from the unrealistic demands required by patriarchal institutionalized motherhood, mothering becomes a site of feminist political activism where mothers consciously bring together their feminism and their parenting to trouble and contest the patriarchal institution of motherhood. Each mother is committed to resisting some of the damaging elements of motherhood, whether they are assumptions about the composition and functioning of family structures and interpersonal relationships within and outside of the family—for example, adhering to suppositions that mothers are heterosexual and/or that heterosexual mothers will happily take on and perform the responsibilities associated with the conjoined roles of wife and mother—or expectations placed on all mothers to engage in and be solely responsible for implementing intensive or sacrificial mothering techniques.

Not only do feminist mothers model alternative ways of practicing mothering for their children and for others, they also intentionally raise their children in ways that challenge patriarchal assumptions about power relations and hierarchies within and outside the family, and practice alternative approaches to, and methods of, mothering that empower them and their children. Through their practice of matroreform, each mother purposely engages in conscious and authentic relationships with her child/ren with the logical intention of effecting positive cultural and political change. For example, as seen in Chapters Two, Three, and Four, all mothers engage in relationships with their sons and daughters that respect their children's human rights, and consciously work to develop relationships with them that are open, honest, and non-hierarchal.

They are also candid about their own understanding of mothering and their relationships with their children. For instance, they have invented and continue to engage in a form of feminist mothering that benefits both mothers and children when mothers live their lives and practice mothering from a position of agency and authority that respects and supports their independence and autonomy both within and outside of mothering. The daughters, too, recognize that feminist mothering is a political act when they reflect upon their mothers' parenting practices, as well as imagine their own (future) mothering decisions in Chapter Four.

Both mothers and daughters share the common belief in and practice of accepting that expectations of each person in the relationship—as well as their mores, values, and perspectives—may differ and/or change over time. They value frank communication and respect each other's right to those ideas and thoughts, as noted in Chapters Two, Three, and Four. The particular approaches to feminist mothering of these women prominently feature maternal power and bestow great worth to mothering through the redefinition and reformation of motherwork as a deeply social and political act.

Feminist Mothering is Messy

The second theme that arises within *Practicing Feminist Mothering* is that these particular approaches to conscious feminist parenting are complicated and, at times, messy for mothers, their children, and others.

Following a feminist tradition of breaking the silence/s around the realities of women's lives, and making space to reflect upon their own experiences of mothering, these feminist mothers speak honestly and share some of the challenges they encounter when engaging in matroreform. By considering the complexities of feminist mothering, they effectively reveal the facade of composure and the supposed ease of motherwork associated with the patriarchal mask of motherhood, identified by Susan Maushart. They also succinctly articulate the ongoing effort intrinsic to the feminist praxis of intentionally uniting feminism and mothering practices in diverse and complex ways.

While the cognitive, affective, and behavioural reformation of mothering that often takes place through the practice of matroreform in feminist mothering can be empowering for mothers and their children, the effort and responsibility of claiming power for themselves and for their children can also be chaotic. Being conscious, reflective, and open with themselves, their children, and at times with others about the decisions they make as mothers takes time, energy, and fortitude that are not always readily available. Managing the tensions they feel among idealized notions of motherhood which, at times, they internalize and battle, their own understandings and visions of mothering, and some of the ways in which they are able to defy the master patriarchal discourse of motherhood, are examples provided in Chapters Two and Three of the messiness of matroreform.

While feminist mothering often creates closeness between mothers and their children, it also generates uncomfortable tensions and contradictions between them. For instance, the voices of mothers in Chapters Two and Three and the reflections of daughters in Chapter Four note how the strain is not an uncommon experience for both daughters and mothers who are in families practicing feminist mothering. Yet, this stress is not limited to mothers and children. Mothers also experience conflict and pressure between themselves and others (teachers, other family members, medical professionals, etc.), and are often on the receiving end of the disparaging gaze of others for their non-conforming parenting practices.

Feelings of isolation, marginalization, lack of support, and guilt associated with the intellectual and psychological energy required in being aware, of understanding, and of consciously explaining, troubling, and reforming the ideology of patriarchal motherhood identified in Chapter Three also point to the tension mothers experience. The work of figuring out the how and why of parenting in ways that are informed by their feminism can also be divisive and frustrating, particularly when dealing with homophobia, racism, classist assumptions, the challenges of living on social assistance, and the work of constantly challenging sexist and misogynist stereotypical depictions of gender and the sexualization of girls and women.

Clearly the process of resistance that feminist mothers employ necessitates making different and often difficult decisions about how they parent and the relationships they engage in with their children and with others. Exposing the construction of patriarchal motherhood, its power, and its damaging regulations and restrictions that endorse the virtues of the stereotypical "good mother" and forewarn the dangers of the "bad mother" can be gruelling. Feelings of "enslavement, victimization, and abuse," as expressed by some of the mothers, articulate the negative repercussions of patriarchal motherhood and the great need to resist, reform, and invent other approaches of mothering that nurture mothers and families.

Although the experiences of feminist mothers who are consciously engaged in the praxis of feminist mothering and the practice of matroreform are fraught with tension and uncomfortable complexity at times, these feminist mothers nevertheless feel compelled and often empowered to reform motherhood and their own mothering, as well as reaffirm their own feminist motherwork by creating feminist motherlines in ways that make it possible for them to raise children who are able to live with/in, yet also contest, the culture of patriarchy.

Change and Continuity

The final theme found in *Practicing Feminist Mothering* is that feminist mothers engage in a practice of mothering that is informed and affected by their explicit intentions of tenaciously valuing and working to create social change through actively bringing feminist praxis into their mothering. They take on the unique challenge of simultaneously engaging in the political act of matroreform and persistently encouraging, respecting, and ensuring continuity through fostering feminist motherlines.

Bringing about change through these two conscious practices of matroreform and feminist motherlines is, I believe, what Deb is suggesting in the quote at the beginning of this final chapter when she claims, "Feminist mothering is a living thing." I understand Deb to be saying that feminist mothering is a responsive, growing, and living practice that continues to have the capacity to reflect upon and critically interact with the world to create meaningful change as it transforms with the passing of time, and that the values, strategies, and practices of that political work can be taught to the next generation, which can continue to modify motherhood and carry on the traditions that are appropriate to support and foster feminist mothering over time. The feminist commitment of these mothers is to bring about social change for themselves and for their children, both within and outside their identities and responsibilities as daughters, parents, and grandparents.

Rather than being a stagnant, mechanical, and formulaic practice, feminist mothering is alive and vibrant as it simultaneously nurtures mothers and children, and contests and challenges the roles, assumptions, and expectations placed on the structure and construction of families and their members by patriarchal motherhood. Whether dealing directly with issues of race and ethnicity like May and Gemma, and Jackie and her son, addressing the complexities and consequences of restricted financial means like Willow, Jackie, and Paula, or articulating, critiquing, and revising the construction and expression of gender and sexuality as Carol, Kim, Shar, and Darcy do, all mothers are aware of their political consciousness as feminists.

Along with Jody, Tammy, Andrea, Beverly, Lynette, Neire, Kim, and Laura, they are explicit about their intentions of uniting their feminism and mothering through feminist praxis in their daily motherwork with their children, families, and others. They are also committed to passing on this knowledge and practice to their children, who they acknowledge may resist, revise, or renew feminist mothering and feminist motherlines in the future.

Questions and Suggestions

As I close *Practicing Feminist Mothering*, I am left with a few questions for both feminism and the field of maternal scholarship to consider. Given the recent issue of the Toronto heterosexual couple and parents, mother Kathy Witterick and father David Stocker, being criticized this spring, particularly from mid May to early June 2011, in the Canadian and British press for raising their third child Storm, age four months, in a "social experiment" to be "genderless" by choosing not to use a gender-specific name or pronoun, and by not disclosing the child's gender to people outside the family, I wonder what role feminism and maternal scholars will play in ensuring that issues such as gender socialization, and identity, along with family and parenting autonomy are discussed rationally and without the patriarchal strategies that victimize, marginalize and stigmatize families who don't conform to or reproduce its narrow ideals.[172]

I also wonder if feminists, maternal scholars, and feminist parents will publicly support such a brave and minority position taken by Witterick and Stocker. I am concerned and admittedly fearful, as are many parents, and particularly mothers who are already vulnerable due to assumptions about their ability to parent should they be assumed to be financially impoverished, under-educated, or illiterate, queer, (dis)abled, or part of a "minority" cultural and religious group, that the well-known legacy of the state will continue to interrogate, judge, and punish families who breach its patriarchal ideals and models of gender and parenting practices. While studying, exploring, and expanding the gender socialization of children has been a focus of academic, activist, and grassroots feminists, and while maternal scholars and feminists recognize that folks who do not meet social expectations, or who contest and/or break social mores and norms around creating families and child-rearing practices, are not "bad" parents, they are still considered to hold a minority opinion. These alternative perspectives must be continually respected, articulated, defended, and fought for, and I hope that feminists and maternal scholars will do so.

Yet, I am optimistic because it seems to me that the important role of feminist parenting through matroreform continues to be alive and evident in the ongoing challenges that families are making to patriarchal motherhood and its norms. The recent case of Kathy Witterick and David Stocker raising baby Storm and their two older sons in ways that support the belief that the sex and gender of children should not determine their place in the world is one example of the way in which families are troubling and countering normative mainstream theories and ideologies of child development and the institution of motherhood. It also speaks to the importance of including their experiences alongside the many developing approaches to matroreform and feminist motherlines.

It is also an example of the messiness of parenting that takes into consideration or is premised on feminism, given that the Witterick/Stocker family is not only the focus of public ridicule but, as a result, is also more likely to be under the scrutiny of social services for their unique parenting methods. Drawing upon the experiences of feminist mothers and their children can assist in challenging the state, whether its police force and judicial system, education and medical structures, or social services with the power to remove children from their family homes, and offer viable family alternatives to the narrowly prescribed ideal patriarchal family unit.

Another disturbing situation requiring the continual attention and response of feminists and maternal scholars is the surge in sexist attitudes and actions of the Canadian judicial system. I am purposely referring to two specific incidents. The first is an international series of protests known as "slut walks" that first took place in Toronto on April 3, 2011, in response to comments made by Toronto Police Constable Michael Sanguinetti in January 2011 during a presentation to a personal security class at York University in Toronto that "women should avoid dressing like sluts in order not to be victimized."[173] The second is the public outrage to the February 18, 2011, decision made by Manitoba Judge Robert Dewar to not give jail time to "clumsy Don Juan" Kenneth Rhodes, who overpowered and raped a 20-year-old woman by the side of a dark and deserted highway in 2006 because "sex was in the air" due to the victim's decision to wear a tube top, high heels, and a lot of makeup that evening.[174]

These sexist comments made by Sanguinetti and Dewar stirred a cacophony of feminist voices, community outrage, and street activism that had not been witnessed for some time. However, while these swift and greatly supported responses by many feminist women, men, and gender queer folks rallying in the streets and calling for the resignation of Constable Sanguinetti and Judge Dewar have drawn mainstream media attention to the issues of violence against women, the same media has been quick to raise questions of, and force debate among feminists about the usefulness of reappropriating the word "slut" as a fundamental cornerstone of contemporary feminist movement and as a useful approach to raising the issue of social attitudes and policies, particularly those related to the police and to the judicial system.[175] By drawing the focus of feminists to the language or term "slut" used in organizing protests, the unacceptable legacy of "slut-shaming" and victim-blaming that needs to stop remains on the periphery and, therefore, continues to be practiced in mainstream media.

Just as in the above case of baby Storm's family, the similar issues of gender socialization, identity, and the autonomy of families and women are either ignored or are aggressively and sceptically questioned. Those who refuse to adhere to and reproduce patriarchal ideals around women's sexuality, sexual behaviour, and gender presentation and performance that are reflected in the Dewar ruling and in Sanguinetti's comments continue to be stigmatized and cast as deviants on the margins who are irrational and potentially dangerous.

The public groundswell of resistance by feminists and others to these sexist and misogynist attitudes is a positive initial response that needs to be maintained by many, including feminists and maternal scholars. Again, I see the praxis of feminist mothering, matroreform, and feminist motherlines as having a role to play here. By ensuring that more people develop and live a feminist consciousness that is able to understand and debate the complexities of issues like these and others regarding autonomy, independence, gender, and sexual identity, feminists, maternal scholars, and feminist mothers are more able to positively contribute to the development and the sustainability of approaches that are intentionally self-reflective and critical of their own perspectives and those of others. This can only assist in a more just, accountable, and responsible society for all of its members, which after all, is a goal of feminist mothering.

By not being a "how-to book" that prescribes a particular or single way of approaching and carrying out feminist mothering, this volume has instead explored a few of the many ways in which feminist mothers may choose to parent, and has made more explicit the feminist mothering practices that have been missing from previous feminist writing on motherhood. Obviously there is not a single, universal feminist way to parent, as mothering practices vary for each family, which may be influenced, but not limited by social class, racialization, (dis)ability, and sexual orientation. However, my conversations with these mothers and daughters offer insight into some of the ways they commonly engage their feminism with their mothering, and constitute an identifiable practice of feminist mothering, which is one way in which feminists are choosing to take on the work and responsibility of uniting feminism and mothering. Feminist mothering for these particular women entails integrating feminism with mothering, explicitly critiquing patriarchal motherhood, and committing to a practice of conscious feminist mothering, which, in this case, engages a cohesive practice of matroreform and developing feminist motherlines for both themselves and their children.

ENDNOTES

1 Together, my partner and I fully agreed to completely support our son's development in this way and together we have modelled an alternative way of parenting as he has matured through boyhood, adolescence, and into adulthood, now at 22 years of age. While I recognize that fathers and other parents involved in raising children have an influence on parenting approaches and on their children, this book nevertheless focuses specifically on feminist mothers, the intersection of their feminism and their mothering, and their personal relationships with their children.

2 Rich, A. 1986. *Of Woman Born: Motherhood as Experience and Institution*. London: Virago, p. 13.

3 See, for instance, Green, F. 2003. "What's Love Got To Do With It? A Personal Reflection on the Role of Maternal Love in Feminist Teaching." *Journal of the Association for Research on Mothering*. 5 (2):47–56; Green, F. 2004. "Feminist Mothers: Successfully Negotiating the Tension Between Motherhood as 'Institution' and 'Experience'" in O'Reilly, A. (Ed.) *From Motherhood to Mothering The Legacy of Adrienne Rich's Of Woman Born*. Albany, SUNY, p. 161–176; Green, F. 2005. "Feminist Mothering: Challenging Gender Inequality by Resisting the Institution of Motherhood and Raising Children to be Critical Agents of Social Change." *Socialist Studies* 1 (1):83–99; Green, F. 2006. "Developing a Feminist Motherline: Reflections on a Decade of Feminist

Parenting." *Journal of the Association for Research on Mothering*. 8 (2):17–20; Green, F. 2008. "Feminist Motherline: Embodied Knowledge/s of Feminist Mothering" in A. O'Reilly (Ed.), *Feminist Mothering*. Albany: SUNY, p. 161–176; Green, F. 2008a. "Matroreform: Feminist Mothers and Their Daughters Creating Feminist Motherlines." *Journal for the Association for Research on Mothering*. 10 (2):11–21; Green, F. 2009. *Feminist Mother in Theory and Practice, 1985–1995*. New York: Mellen Press; Green, F. 2011. Feminist Maternal Pedagogies: Inside and Outside the Classroom in D. Byrd and F. Green (Eds.), *Maternal Pedagogies: In and Outside the Classroom*. Toronto: Demeter Press, 197-211.

4 Mothers can also feel empowered without enacting feminism, as noted by Erika Horwitz in *Through the Maze of Motherhood Empowered Mothers Speak*; however, the focus here is on the intersection of feminism and mothering, and how it assists in the empowerment of feminist mothers and their children.

5 Fonow, M. & Cook, J. 1991. "Back to the Future: A Look at the Second Wave of Feminist Epistemology and Methodology" in M. Fonow & J. Cook (Eds.), *Beyond Methodology: Feminist Scholarship as Lived Research*. (1–15). Indianapolis: Indiana University Press; Harding, S. 1987. "Introduction" in S. Harding (Ed.), *Feminism and Methodology Social Science Issues*. (1–14). Milton Keynes: Open University Press; Reinharz, S. 1992. *Feminist Methods in Social Research*. Oxford: Oxford University Press; Stanley, L. 1990. *Feminist Praxis: Research, Theory and Epistemology in Feminist Sociology*. New York: Routledge; Stacey, J. 1993. "Untangling Feminist Theory" in D. Richardson & V. Robinson (Eds.), *Thinking Feminist: Key Concepts in Women's Studies*. New York: Guilford Press, p. 49–73; Stanley, L., & Wise, S. 1993. *Breaking Out Again: Feminist Ontology and Epistemology*. London: Routledge.

6 Kirby, S. & McKenna, K. 1989. *Experience, Research, Social Change: Methods from the Margins*. Toronto: Garamond Press; Kirby, S., Greaves, L. and Reid, C. 2006. *Experience, Research, Social Change: Methods Beyond the Mainstream*. Peterborough, ON: Broadview Press.

7 Glaser, B. 1978. *Theoretical Sensitivity: Advances in the Methodology of Grounded Theory*. Mill Valley, Ca: Sociology Press; Glaser, B. 1992. *Basics of Grounded Theory Analysis: Emergence vs. Forcing*. Mill Valley, Ca.: Sociology Press; Glaser, B. 1998. *Doing Grounded Theory: Issues and Discussions*. Mill Valley, Ca.: Sociology Press; Glaser, B., & Strauss, A. 1967. *The Discovery of Grounded Theory: Strategies for Qualitative Research*. Chicago: Aldine Publishing Co.; Strauss, A. & Corbin, J. 1990. *The Basics of Qualitative Research: Grounded Theory Procedures and Techniques*. London: Sage; Strauss, A. & Corbin, J. 1994. "Grounded Theory Methodology: An Overview" in D. Norman& Y. Lincoln (Eds.), *Handbook of Qualitative Research*. (273–285). London: Sage Publications; Strauss, A. & Corbin, J. 1997. *Grounded Theory in Practice*. Thousand Oakes, CA: Sage.; Strauss, A. & Corbin, J. 2007. *Basics of Qualitative Research Techniques and Procedures for Developing Grounded Theory*. Third Edition. Thousand Oakes, CA: Sage.

8 Subjectivity here refers to "the description or interpretation of an experience from the perspective or position of the person engaged within the experience" while subjugated knowledge/s refers to "the trivialized or discredited knowledge that is lost or silenced as a result of circulating outside of the accepted boundaries of the master narrative or universal discourse (patriarchal)" (Abbey & O'Reilly, 1998:334); Waring (1994).

9 Wong-Wylie, G. 2006. "Images and Echoes in Matroreform: A Cultural Feminist Perspective." *Journal for the Association for Research on Mothering* 8 (1&2):135.

10 Green, F. 2006. "Developing a Feminist Motherline: Reflections on a Decade of Feminist Parenting." *Journal of the Association for Research on Mothering*. 8 (2):17–20.

11 Taylor, D. 1997. "Overview: The Uneasy Relationship between Motherhood and Feminism" in Jettner, A., Orleck, A. and Taylor, D. (Eds.), *The Politics of Motherhood: Activist Voices from Left to Right*. Hanover: University Press of New England, p. 350.

12 Hirsch, M. 1997. "Feminism at the Maternal Divide: A Diary" in A. Jetter, A. Orleck & D. Taylor (Eds.), *The Politics of Motherhood: Activist Voices from Left to Right*. Hanover: University Press of New England, p. 353.

13 Freely, M. 1995. *What About Us? An Open Letters to the Mothers Feminism Forgot*. London: Bloomsberg, p. 1.

14 Anderson, K. 2000. *A Recongniton of Being: Reconstructin Native Motherhood*. Toronto: Second Story Press; Anderson, K. 2007. "Giving Life to the People: An Indigenous Ideology of Motherhood" in O'Reilly, A. (Ed). *Maternal Theory: Essential Readings*. Toronto: Demeter Press, p. 761–781; Driver, S. & Newman Z. 2011. *Queer Parenting*. Toronto, Demeter Press; Epstein, R. 2009. *Who's Your Daddy And Other Writings On Queer Parenting*. Sumach Press; Forcey, Linda Rennie. 1999. "Book Review." *Signs*. Vol. 25(1):301; Kline, M. 2000. "Complicating the Ideology of Motherhood: Child Welfare Law and First Nation Women" in B. Crow & L. Gotell (Eds.), *Open Boundaries: A Canadian Women's Studies Reader*. Toronto: Prentice Hall, p. 194–204; Lavell-Harvard, M. and Corbeire Lavell, J. (Eds). 2006. *Until Our Hearts Are on the Ground: Aboriginal Mothering, Oppression, Resistance and Rebirth*. Toronto: Demeter Press; Kuttai, H. 2010. *Maternity Rolls: Pregnancy, Childbirth and Disability. Halifax: Fernwood Press*; Mullins, A. 2005. *Reconceiving Pregnancy and Childcare: Ethics, Experience, and Reproductive Labor*. Cambridge: Cambridge University Press; Snitow, A. 1992. "Feminism and Motherhood: An American Reading." *Feminist Review*. Vol. 40:34.

15 For discussion on motherhood by feminist foremothers see: Benn, M. 1998. *Madonna and Child: Towards a New Politics of Motherhood*. London: Jonathan Cape; Freely, M. 1995. *What About Us? An Open Letters to the Mothers Feminism Forgot*. London: Bloomsberg; Hamilton, R. 1990. "Feminism and Motherhood, 1970–1990: Reinventing the Wheel?" RFR/DRF, 19 (3/4), p. 23–31; Hirsch, M. 1997. "Feminism at the Maternal Divide: A Diary" in Jettner, A., Orleck, A. and Taylor, D. (Eds.), *The Politics of Motherhood: Activist*

Voices from Left to Right. Hanover: University Press of New England, p. 352–368; Umansky, L. 1996. *Motherhood Reconceived: Feminism and the Legacies of the Sixties*. New York: New York University Press.

16 For instance, I draw on Bashevkin, S. 1994. "Confronting Neo-conservatism: Anglo-American Women's Movements under Thatcher, Reagan and Mulroney." *International Political Science Review*. Vo. 15 (3):275–296; Benn, M. 1998. *Madonna and Child: Towards a New Politics of Motherhood*. London: Jonathan Cape; Hirsch, M. 1989. *The Mother/Daughter Plot: Narrative, Psychoanalysis, Feminism*. Bloomington: Indiana University Press; Hirsch, M. 1997. "Feminism at the Maternal Divide: A Diary" in Jettner, A., Orleck, A. and Taylor, D. (Eds.), *The Politics of Motherhood: Activist Voices from Left to Right*. Hanover: University Press of New England, p. 352–368. O'Brien Hallstein, L. D. 2008. "Second Wave Silences and Third Wave Intensive Mothering" in A. Kinser (Ed.), *Mothering in the Third Wave*. Toronto: Demeter Press, p. 107–118. Snitow, A. 1992. "Feminism and Motherhood: An American Reading." *Feminist Review*. Vol. 40:32–51; Tucker, J. Stadtman. 2006. "Care as a Cause: Framing the Twenty-First-Century Mother's Movement" in M. Hamington and D. Miller (Eds.), *Socializing Care: Feminist Ethics and Public Issues*. New York: Rowman & Littlefield Publishers, p. 183–203.

17 Hirsch, M. 1997. p. 349.

18 Green, F. 2010. "Patriarchal Ideology of Motherhood" in A. O'Reilly (Ed.), *Encyclopedia on Motherhood*. Sage Press, p. 969–970.

19 Green, F. 2009. *Feminist Mother in Theory and Practice, 1985–1995*. New York: Mellen Press, p. 91–92; Johnson, M. 1988. *Strong Mothers, Weak Wives*. Berkeley: University of California Press; Hallstein, L. D. 2008. "Second Wave Silences and Third Wave Intensive Mothering" in A. Kinser (Ed.), *Mothering in the Third Wave*. (107–118) Toronto: Demeter Press, p. 108; Mack-Canty, C. & Wright, S. 2008. "Parenting in Third Wave Feminism and Empowering All

Family Members" in A. O'Reilly (Ed.), *Feminist Mothering*. Albany: SUNY, p. 144; Okin, S. 1989. *Justice, Gender and the Family*. New York: Basic Books; Taylor, D. 1997, "Overview: The Uneasy Relationship between Motherhood and Feminism" in Jettner, A., Orleck, A. and Taylor, D. (Eds.), *The Politics of Motherhood: Activist Voices from Left to Right*. Hanover: University Press of New England, p. 349.

20 Davin, A. 1978. Imperialism and Motherhood. *History Workshop*. Vol.5:14.

21 Snitow, A. 1992. "Feminism and Motherhood: An American Reading." *Feminist Review*. Vol. 40:33.

22 Benn, M. 1998: *Madonna and Child: Towards a New Politics of Motherhood*. London: Jonathan Cape, p. 232.

23 Scarth, F. 2004. *The Other Within: Ethics, Politics and the Body in Simone de Beauvoir*. Lanham and Oxford: Rowman & Littlefield, p. 138.

24 Heywood, A. 2003. *Political Ideologies: An Introduction*. Palgrave Macmillan, p. 272; Sydie, R. A. 1994. Natural Women, Cultured Men: A Feminist Perspective On Sociological Theory. Vancouver: University of British Columbia Press, p. 143–148.

25 Snitow, A. 1992. p. 36–37.

26 Benn, M. 1998. *Madonna and Child: Towards a New Politics of Motherhood*. London: Jonathan Cape, Chapter 10; Freely, M. 1995. *What About Us? An Open Letters to the Mothers Feminism Forgot*. London: Bloomsberg; Hirsch, M. 1997. "Feminism at the Maternal Divide: A Diary" in Jettner, A., Orleck, A. and Taylor, D. (Eds.), *The Politics of Motherhood: Activist Voices from Left to Right*. Hanover: University Press of New England, p. 354.

27 Benn, M. 1998. p. 218.

28 Benn, M. 1998. p. 191.

29 Hallstein, L. D. 2008. "Second Wave Silences and Third Wave Intensive Mothering" In Kinser, A. (Ed.), *Mothering in the Third Wave*. Toronto: Demeter Press, p. 117; Snitow, A. 1992. "Feminism and Motherhood: An American Reading."

Feminist Review. Vol. 40:37; Umansky, L. 1996. *Motherhood Reconceived: Feminism and the Legacies of the Sixties*. New York: New York University Press.

30 Hirsch, M. 1997. "Feminism at the Maternal Divide: A Diary" in Jettner, A., Orleck, A. and Taylor, D. (Eds.), *The Politics of Motherhood: Activist Voices from Left to Right*. Hanover: University Press of New England, p. 355; Hallstein, L. D. 2008. "Second Wave Silences and Third Wave Intensive Mothering" in A. Kinser (Ed.), *Mothering in the Third Wave*. Toronto: Demeter Press, p. 107–118.

31 Hirsch, M. 1997. p. 356.

32 Hallstein, L. D. 2008. "Second Wave Silences and Third Wave Intensive Mothering" in A. Kinser (Ed.), *Mothering in the Third Wave*. Toronto: Demeter Press, p. 110.

33 Morgan, R. 1978. *Going Too Far: The Personal Chronicle of a Feminist*. New York: Vintage, p. 8.

34 Hirsch, M. 1997. p. 360–1.

35 Hirsch, M. 1997. p. 360.

36 See, for instance, Glenn, E. 1994. "Social Constructions of Mothering: A Thematic Overview" in Glen, E., Chang, G. & Forcey, L. (Eds.), *Mothering: Ideology, Experience, and Agency*. (1–29) New York: Routledge; Collins, P. 1987. The Meaning of Motherhood in Black Culture and Black Mother/Daughter Relationships. *Sage: A Scholarly Journal on Black Women*. 1 (2):3–10; Collins, P. 1989. "The Social Construction of Black Feminist Thought." *Signs Journal for Women in Culture and Society*. 14 (41):745–773; and Orleck, A. 1997. "Tradition Unbound: Radical Mothers in International Perspective" in Jettner, A., Orleck, A. and Taylor, D. (Eds.). *The Politics of Motherhood: Activist Voices from Left to Right*. Hanover: University Press of New England, p. 5.

37 Hirsch, M. 1997. p. 365.

38 Taylor, D. 1997. p. 350.

39 Hirsch, M. 1981. "Mothers and Daughters." *Signs*. Vol. 7 (1):203. Jessie Bernard followed this first book with a second in 1976, entitled *Women, Wives and Mothers: Values and Options*.

40 Hirsch, M. 1997. p. 357.

41 Susan Faludi makes a similar argument with regard to the common trend wihin American feminist movement of dissociating from the previous generation of feminists and feminism in the 2010 *Harper's Magazine* article "American Electra: Feminism's Ritual Matricide."

42 Benn, M. 1998. *Madonna and Child: Towards a New Politics of Motherhood*. London: Jonathan Cape, 220; Hirsch, M. 1997. "Feminism at the Maternal Divide: A Diary" in Jettner, A., Orleck, A. and Taylor, D. (Eds.), *The Politics of Motherhood: Activist Voices from Left to Right*. Hanover: University Press of New England, p. 358.

43 Courses in Women's Studies were taught across Canada since the early 1970s. The University of Winnipeg, for instance, started teaching its first courses in Women's Studies in 1979 and became a program offering its first degree by 1987.

44 Some of these authors include Jessica Benjamin (1988), Nancy Chodorow (1978), Helen Cixous (1986), Dorothy Dinnerstein (1976), Jane Flax (1978), Carol Gilligan (1982), Luce Irigaray (1981; 1985), Evelyn Fox Keller (1985), Jayne Lazarre (1978), and Adrienne Rich (1976).

45 Benn, M. 1998. p. 220.

46 Hirsch, M. 1981. "Mothers and Daughters." *Signs*. Vol. 7 (1):209.

47 Hirsch, M. 1997. p. 358–9.

48 Hirsch, M. 1997. p. 361.

49 Benn, M. 1998. *Madonna and Child: Towards a New Politics of Motherhood*. London: Jonathan Cape, 219; Hirsch, M. 1981. "Mothers and Daughters." *Signs*. Vol. 7 (1):208.

50 Hirsch, M. 1997. p. 358–9.

51 Snitow, A. 1992. "Feminism and Motherhood: An American Reading." *Feminist Review*. Vol. 40:38–39.

52 Hirsch, M. 1981. "Mothers and Daughters." *Signs*. Vol. 7 (1):220.

53 Hirsch, M. 1981..

54 Ruddick, S. 1995. *Maternal Thinking: Toward a Politics of Peace*. Boston: Beacon Press, p. xi.

55 Hirsch, M. 1997. p. 361–2.

56 See, for example: Elizabeth Badinter (1981), Ann Dally (1982); Hester Eisenstein (1983), Ann Ferguson (1989), Barbara Rothman (1989), Joyce Treblicot (1983), and Betsy Wearing (1984).

57 Bashevkin, S. 1994. "Confronting Neo-conservatism: Anglo-American Women's Movements under Thatcher, Reagan, and Mulroney." *International Political Science Review*. Vo. 15 (3):275–296; Begin, M. 1992. "The Royal Commission on the Status of Women in Canada: Twenty Years Later" in C. Backhouse & D. H. Flaherty (Eds.), *Changing Times*. Montreal: McGill-Queen's University Press, p. 37.

58 According to the NORAD official website, "The North American Aerospace Defense Command (NORAD) is a United States and Canada bi-national organization charged with the missions of aerospace warning and aerospace control for North America. Aerospace warning includes the monitoring of man-made objects in space, and the detection, validation, and warning of attack against North America whether by aircraft, missiles, or space vehicles, through mutual support arrangements with other commands" <www.norad.mil/about/index.html>. Bashevkin, S. 1994. "Confronting Neo-conservatism: Anglo-American Women's Movements Under Thatcher, Reagan, and Mulroney." *International Political Science Review*. Vo. 15 (3):275–296; Begin, M. 1992. "The Royal Commission on the Status of Women in Canada: Twenty Years Later" in C. Backhouse & D. H. Flaherty (Eds.), *Changing Times*. Montreal: McGill-Queen's University Press, p. 37; Rebick. J. 2005. *Ten Thousand Roses: The Making of a Feminist Revolution*. Toronto: Penguin, p. 126–218.

59 Bashevkin, S. 1994. Confronting Neo-conservatism: Anglo-American Women's Movements under Thatcher, Reagan and Mulroney. *International Political Science Review*. Vo. 15 (3):275–296; Begin, M. 1992. "The Royal Commission on the Status of Women in Canada: Twenty Years Later" in

C. Backhouse & D. H. Flaherty (Eds.), *Changing Times*. Montreal: McGill-Queen's University Press, p. 37; Rebick. J. 2005. *Ten Thousand Roses: The Making of a Feminist Revolution*. Toronto: Penguin, p. 126–218.

60 Young, L. & Cross, W. 2003. "Women and Conservative Parties in Canada and the United States" in Schultze, R-O, Sturm, R., and Eberle, D. (Eds.). *Conservative Parties and Right Wing Politics in North America: Mapping the Benefits of an Ideological Victory*? Druck: DruckPartner Rubelmann, Hemsbach, Germany, p. 207.

61 Young, L. & Cross, W. 2003. "Women and Conservative Parties in Canada and the United States" in Schultze, R-O, Sturm, R., and Eberle, D. (Eds.). *Conservative Parties and Right Wing Politics in North America: Mapping the Benefits of an Ideological Victory*? Druck: DruckPartner Rubelmann, Hemsbach, Germany, p. 216; Rebick. J. 2005. *Ten Thousand Roses: The Making of a Feminist Revolution*. Toronto: Penguin, p. 126–218.

62 By the 1990s the Alliance was more formally connected with REAL Women and the Christian organization Canadian Action Family Coalition than the Conservatives had been, and increased their efforts to move forward policies to support traditional heterosexual married couples and their children, and actively not support single-parent families, child care, and working women. In 2003, the Alliance Party merged with the Progressive Conservatory Party of Canada, which was in power from 2006–2011 under the leadership of Steven Harper. At the time of writing this chapter, Prime Minister Stephen Harper had just been re-elected in the first majority Conservative government since 1988 to serve a four-year term. See: Young, L. & Cross, W. 2003. "Women and Conservative Parties in Canada and the United States" In Schultze, R-O, Sturm, R., and Eberle, D. (Eds.). *Conservative Parties and Right Wing Politics in North America: Mapping the Benefits of an Ideological Victory*? Druck: DruckPartner Rubelmann, Hemsbach, Germany, p. 218; Rebick. J. 2005. *Ten Thousand Roses: The Making of a Feminist Revolution*. Toronto: Penguin, p. 126–218.

63 Hirsch, M. 1997. p. 361

64 Hirsch, M. 1997. p. 361–2.

65 Dill, B. T. 1988. "Our Mother's Grief: Racial Ethnic Women and the Maintenance of Families." *Journal of Family History*. Vol. 13:415–431;Hirsch, M. 1997. "Feminism at the Maternal Divide: A Diary" in A. Jetter, A. Orleck & D. Taylor (Eds.), *The Politics of Motherhood: Activist Voices from Left to Right*. Hanover: University Press of New England, p. 364.

66 Benn, M. 1998. *Madonna and Child: Towards a New Politics of Motherhood*. London: Jonathan Cape, p. 224; Faludi, S. 1991. *Backlash: The Undeclared War Against American Women*; Snitow, A. 1992. "Feminism and Motherhood: An American Reading." *Feminist Review*. Vol. 40:41.

67 Tucker, J. Stadtman. 2006. "Care as a Cause: Framing the Twenty-First-Century Mother's Movement" in M. Hamington and D. Miller (Eds.), *Socializing Care: Feminist Ethics and Public Issues*. New York: Rowman & Littlefield Publishers, p. 188.

68 Benn, M. 1998. p. 211.

69 Snitow, A. 1992. "Feminism and Motherhood: An American Reading." *Feminist Review*. Vol. 40:41.

70 Benn, M. 1998. p. 212.

71 Benn, M. 1998. p. 212.

72 Benn, M. 1998. p. 227.

73 Benn, M. 1998. p. 228.

74 Benn, M. 1998. p. 228.

75 Tucker, J. Stadtman. 2006. "Care as a Cause: Framing the Twenty-First-Century Mother's Movement" in M. Hamington and D. Miller (Eds.), *Socializing Care: Feminist Ethics and Public Issues*. New York: Rowman & Littlefield Publishers, p. 183–4.

76 Hirsch, M. 1997. "Feminism at the Maternal Divide: A Diary" in A. Jetter, A. Orleck & D. Taylor (Eds.), *The Politics of Motherhood: Activist Voices from Left to Right*.

Hanover: University Press of New England, p. 364. Snitow, A. 1992. "Feminism and Motherhood: An American Reading." *Feminist Review*. Vo. 40:33.

77 Hirsch, M. 1997. p. 366.

78 Hirsch, M. 1997. p. 366.

79 Faludi, S. 2010. American Electra: Feminism's ritual matricide. *Harper's Magazine*. October: 29–42; Hirsch, M. 1997. p. 365.

80 Investigation in the role of science and child rearing experts continued into the 21st century with books such as *Perfect Motherhood: Science and Childrearing in America* by Rima Apple (2006) and *Raising America: Experts, Parents and a Century of Advice about Children* by Ann Hulbert (2003).

81 Johnston, D. & Swanson, D. 2003. "Invisible Mothers: A Content Analysis of Motherhood Ideologies and Myths in Magazines." *Sex Roles*. Vol. 49 (1/2):21–33; Kuperberg, A. & Stone, P. 2008. "The Media Depiction of Women Who Opt Out." *Gender and Society*. Vol. 22(4):497–517; Smith, A. 2001. "Mass-market Magazine Portrayals of Working Mothers and other Related Issues, 1987 and 1997." *Journal of Children and Poverty*. Vol. 7:101–119.

82 Benn, M. 1998. p. 232.

83 Child care in Canada falls under provincial jurisdiction and includes the power to implement public child-care programs; permit or prohibit private child care providers; regulate the type of services child care facilities will provide, and; dictate the type of education and certification child care professionals must have to provide their services. Provincial governments also have the constitutional power to provide financial benefits in the area of child care, which may include provincial tax credits and direct subsidies to child-care providers to reduce the cost of child care for parents. <www.mapleleafweb.com/features/child-care-canada-introduction#canadian>.

84 Glenn et al. (Eds.), 1994. "Preface." *Mothering: Ideology, Experience, and Agency*. New York: Routledge, p. ix.

85 Hays, S. 1998. *The Cultural Contradictions of Motherhood*. New Haven: Yale University Press, p. 54.

86 See, for example, Boesveld (2009). The debate around the parenting strategies used and described by mother and Yale law professor Amy Chua in her 2011 book *Battle Hymn of the Tiger Mother* is one such example. Others include the criticism given to "helicopter parents" for hovering over their children and to "soccer moms" for being pushy and aggressive as they try to serve the best interests of their children, and critical of mothers who work outside of the home for a living. See the following for more inforation: Barton, A. 2010. "Smother Mothers: Give Helicopter Parents A Break." *Globe and Mail. Globe Life*. Sunday, July 25. <www.theglobeandmail.com/life/family-and-relationships/give-helicopter-parents-a-break/article1651532/>; Button, L. No date. "Helicopter Parents." *ParentsCanada.com*. <www.parentscanada.com/developing/tweens/articles.aspx?listingid=312>; Gibbs, N. 2009. "The Growing Backlash Against Overparenting." *Time*. Friday, November 20. <www.time.com/time/nation/article/0,8599,1940395,00.html>.

87 See, for example: Friedman, M. & Calizte, L. (Eds). 2009. *Mothering and Blogging: The Radical Act of the MommyBlog*. Toronto: Demeter Press.

88 Crittenden, A. 2002. *The Price of Motherhood: Why The Most Important Job In The World Is Still The Least Valued*. New York: Owl Books, back jacket cover.

89 The creation and birth of ARM/MIRCI was in response to two hugely successful international conferences on mothering and motherhood co-coordinated by Dr. Andrea O'Reilly and sponsored by the Centre for Feminist Research (CFR) at York University, Toronto, Ontario, Canada. The original international conference on "Mothers and Daughters: Moving into the Next Millennium" was held in September 1997 at York University. Over 150 women from Canada, the United States, and Europe attended with great interest and enthusiasm. This motivated Dr. O'Reilly and the CFR to host a second international mothering conference, "Mothers and Sons

Today: Challenges and Possibilities" a year later in 1998, and to launch ARM/MIRCI. Also committed to community building for mothers, MIRCI hosts Mother Outlaws activities, which are community gatherings in the Toronto area for women interested in discussing current motherhood issues from a feminist perspective and in sharing the links between their own mothering practices and social change. Mother Outlaw members often gather in each other's homes to share a potluck dinner and informal discussion on a specific topic, or meet at scheduled public special events. For further information on MIRCI, see: Green, F. 2010. "Association for Research on Motherhood" in A. O'Reilly & G. Golsen (Eds.), *Encyclopedia on Motherhood*. Sage Press, p. 85–86.

90 The ARM and MIRCI Journal also feature poetry, photography, and artwork in an effort to give voice to women's lived experiences of mothering in all their complexity and diversity.

91 While a conference on mothering was hosted by the Fort Gary Women's Resource Centre in Winnipeg in the late 1980s, the first annual academic conference on mothering hosted by Dr. Andrea O'Reilly of the Women's Studies Department at York University in Ontario, Canada, did not take place until 1997.

92 This increase in maternal scholarship is primarily due to the relentless work of Canadian motherhood scholar Dr. Andrea O'Reilly, founder of MIRCI (formerly ARM, the Association for Research on Mothering 1998–2010), founding editor and editor-in-chief of *JMI*, (formerly *JARM*, *The Journal of the Association for Research on Mothering* 1999–2010) and founder of Demeter Press in 2004. For further information on Demeter Press, see: Green, F. 2010. "Demeter Press" in A. O'Reilly (Ed.), *Encyclopedia on Motherhood*. p. 279. Sage Press; <demeterpress.org/>. Selected titles of Demeter Press include Jeanette Lavell and Dawn Lavell-Harvard's *Aboriginal Mothering*, (2006), Frances Latchford's *Adoption and Mothering* (2010), Susan Driver and Zoë Newman's *Queer Parenting* (2011), May Friedman and Shana Calixte's *Mothering and Blogging* (2009), and Amber Kinser's *Mothering in the Third Wave* (2008).

93 MOM expects to build a grounded museum in Manhattan, New York, during the second decade of the 2000s. For more information visit <www.museumofmotherhood.org>.

94 O'Reilly, A. 2008a. "Introduction" in A. O'Reilly (Ed.), *Feminist Mothering*. Albany: SUNY, p. 2.

95 Back cover, O'Reilly, A. (Ed.), 2008. *Feminist Mothering*. Albany: SUNY.

96 Kinser, A. 2010a. "Introduction" in A. Kinser (Ed.), *Mothering in the Third Wave*. Toronto: Demeter Press, p. 5.

97 Kinser, A. 2010a. p. 6. An example of this approach can be found in various articles in Daisy Hernadez and Bushra Rehman's 2002 edited collection *Colonize This! Young Women of Color on Today's Feminism*. New York: Seal.

98 Earlier publications by Green addressing feminism and mothering include 1999, 2004, 2006, 2008, 2008, and 2008a.

99 Kinser, A. 2008a. "Mothering as Relational Consciousness" in Andrea O'Reilly (Ed.), *Feminist Mothering* (123–140). Toronto: Demeter Press, p. 123.

100 O'Reilly, A. 2008a. p. 7.

101 Green, F. 2009. *Feminist Mother in Theory and Practice, 1985–1995*. New York: Mellen Press; O'Reilly, A. 2008a. "Introduction" in A. O'Reilly (Ed.), *Feminist Mothering*. Albany: SUNY, p. 7.

102 Green, F. 2009. *Feminist Mother in Theory and Practice, 1985–1995*. New York: Mellen Press; Green, F. 2006. "Developing a Feminist Motherline: Reflections on a Decade of Feminist Parenting." *Journal of the Association for Research on Mothering*. 8 (2):17–20.Green, F. 2005. "Feminist Mothering: Challenging Gender Inequality by Resisting the Institution of Motherhood and Raising Children to be Critical Agents of Social Change." *Socialist Studies* Vol. 1 (1):83–99; Green, F. 1999. "Living Feminism Through Mothering" *Journal for the Association of Research on Mothering*. 1 (1):99–104.

103 Green, F. 2009. *Feminist Mother in Theory and Practice, 1985–1995*. New York: Mellen Press; O'Reilly, A. 2008a.

"Introduction" in O'Reilly, A. (Ed.), *Feminist Mothering*. Albany: SUNY, p.8–9.

104 A comment made during an interview in 2005 by Tammy, a 46-year-old, Euro-Canadian, heterosexual, married, mother of three children age 18, 15, and seven years.

105 Code, L. 1991. *What Can She Know? Feminist Theory and the Construction of Knowledge*. Ithaca, New York: Cornell University Press.

106 Abbey, S. 1999. "Researching Motherhood as a Feminist." *Journal of the Association for Research on Mothering*, p. 47, 53. Amber Kinser, 2008a. "Mothering as Relational Consciousness" in O'Reilly, A. (Ed.), *Feminist Mothering*. Toronto: Demeter Press, p. 123.

107 Kirby and McKenna define praxis as "the integration of knowing and doing." Kirby, S. & McKenna, K. 1989. *Experience, Research, Social Change: Methods from the Margins*. Toronto: Garamond Press, p. 34. For further discussion on praxis see: Harcourt, W. 2006. *Feminist Praxis: Women's Transnational and Place Based Struggles for Change*. Great Transition Initiative Paper Series, Frontiers of a Great Change 11, Boston: Tellus Institute for a Great Transition, p. 4.; O'Brien, M. 1981. *The Politics of Reproduction*. London: Routledge & Kegan Paul, 4; Weiner, G. 1994. *Feminisms in Education: an introduction*. Buckingham: Open University Press, p. 121.

108 I use the term "temporarily able-bodied" to highlight the reality that many people will become disabled at some point in their lives through the virtue of aging, or by accident or illness. Being able-bodied is not a permanent condition, but rather one that is temporary. Susan Wendell (1989) addresses this perspective of (dis)ability in Wendell, S. 1989. "Toward a Feminist Theory of Disability." *Hypatia*. 4 (2), 104–124.

109 For further discussion on this particular research see Green, F. 2006. "Developing a Feminist Motherline: Reflections on a Decade of Feminist Parenting." *Journal of the Association for Research on Mothering*. 8 (2):17–20.

110 bell hooks expands upon the astute observation made by French existentialist philosopher Simone de Beauvoir in *The Second Sex* that "one is *not born* a *woman*, but rather becomes one."; hooks, b. *Feminism is for Everybody: Passionate Politics*. New York: South End Press. 2000:7.

111 The excerpts have been slightly modified to assist in an easier flow of dialogue without detracting from its meaning. For further details about the 16 feminist mothers, see Green, F. 2009. *Feminist Mother in Theory and Practice, 1985–1995*. New York: Mellen Press.

112 Abby, S. 1999. Researching Motherhood as a Feminist: Reflecting on My Own Experiences. *Journal of the Association of Research on Mothering*. 1(1):46.

113 Mack-Canty, C. & Wright, S. 2008. "Parenting in Third Wave Feminism and Empowering All Family Members" in O'Reilly, A. (Ed.), *Feminist Mothering*. Albany: SUNY, p. 145.

114 Forna, A. 1999. *Mother of All Myths: How Society Moulds and Constrains Mothers*. London: Harper Collins, p. 24.

115 Rich, A. 1986. *Of Woman Born: Motherhood as Experience and Institution*. London: Virago Press, p.13. Many feminist theorists have followed Rich's initial theorizing and conducted careful historical and sociological work to demonstrate how motherhood is an institution. See for example: Arnup (1990, 1994); Barrett (1988); Kaplan (1992, 1993); Lewis (1990) and Ursel (1992). Other feminist theorists have addressed the patriarchal control of women and mothers in psychology, medicine, popular culture, literature, law, and social policy. See Apple (1995); Arnup (1994); Badinter (1986); Dally (1982); Davin (1978); Glen (1994); Lewis (1980); Oakley (1986); Richardson (1993); Rothman (1989); Schutze (1987); Thurer (1994); Turnbull (2001). For dialogue and research exploring numerous myths, ideologies, and social policies that support the institution of motherhood and have also been influenced by Rich's work see: Anderson (2000); Barrett (1988); Collins (1991); Crawford (1987); Dally (1982); Davies and Welsh (1986); Ferguson (1989); Gieve (1987); Glenn et al. (1994); Gordon (1990); Grupo

Feminista Miercoloes (1980); Hill (1987); Hoffnung (1989); Kline (2000); Knowles and Cole (1990); Lorde (1987); Maroney (1985); Oakley (1986); Pollack (1990); Richardson (1993); Thurer (1994); Ursel (1992) and Wearing (1984).

116 Rich, A. 1986. p. 274–5.

117 Rich, A. 1986. p. 275–6

118 Rich, A. 1986. p. 42.

119 Dr. Gina Wong-Wylie and Russell-Mayhew, S. 2010. "No 'Body' to Blame?: Sociocultural Influences On Girls And Women" in L. Ross (Ed.). *Counselling Women: Feminist Issues, Theory and Practice*, p. 200. Canadian Scholars' Press/ Women's Press.

120 See, for instance, Adrienne Rich, Betty Friedan, and Gina Wong-Wylie for further discussion on the intersectionality of good woman and wife.

121 Pharr, S. 1997. *Homophobia: A Weapon of Sexism*. Expanded Edition. Arizona: Chardon Press, p. 59.

122 Pharr, S. 1997. p. 59.

123 O'Reilly, A. (Ed.). 2004a. "Introduction" in *Mother Outlaws: Theories and Practices of Empowered Mothering*. Toronto: Women's Press, p. 14.

124 Chase, S. and Rogers, M. 2001. *Mothers and Children: Feminist Analysis and Personal Narratives*. NJ: Rutgers University Press, p. 14.

125 Chase, S. and Rogers, M. 2001. p. 14.

126 The code of the bad mother stands in for real confrontations with serious problems of society and avoids looking at poverty, racism, and colonialism, the lack of access to affordable daycare, anti-feminism, devaluation of mothering, and work structures that don't recognize families and child rearing (Ladd-Taylor & Umansky, 1998:23). Weill Cornell Medical College Professor of Psychology, Richard Friedman, notes in a 2010 *Globe and Mail* article that mental health professionals have been trained over time to see a bad mother behind the bad behaviour of children.

127 Statistics Canada. 2006a. "Mother's Day...By the Numbers." <www42.statcan.ca/smr08/2006/smr08_047_2006-eng.htm>.

128 In 2006, women still made up the large majority (80%) of lone parents in Canada. That year, there were a total of 1.1 million female-headed lone-parent families in Canada, which have historically been among the most economically disadvantaged families in the country. While the overall growth rate in the number of lone-parent families has moderated in the past decade, these families continue to account for a relatively large share of all children in Canada. For example, 18% of all children under age 15 lived with a lone parent. For more information see Statistics Canada's "Census Snapshot of Canada—Families" <www.statcan.gc.ca/pub/11-008-x/2007006/article/10380-eng.htm>.

129 At the beginning of the 21st century the term "queer parent" replaced the term "lesbian mothering" to reflect the integration of the shifting parameters of parenting and family beyond hetero-normative boundaries within contemporary critically queer theoretical perspectives that rethink and articulate a range of knowledges and changing embodied parental experiences that include dynamic gender and sexual arrangements as they are lived through multi-layered racial, national, and class relations.

130 A comment made about motherhood during an interview in 2005 with Jody, the 46-year-old, divorced, heterosexual, middle-class, Euro-Canadian mother of an 14-year-old son and a 12-year-old daughter.

131 In 1997, there were 225 divorces per 100,000 people in Canada and 230.9 divorces per 100,000 people in Manitoba (Statistics Canada, 2000).

132 Ladd-Taylor, M. and Umansky, L. (Eds.). 1998. *"Bad" Mothers: The Politics of Blame in Twentieth-Century America*. New York: New York University Press; Waldman, A. 2009. *Bad Mother: A Chronicle of Maternal Crimes, Minor Calamities, and Occasional Moments of Grace*. New York: Doubleday Press.

133 See, for example: Arnup (1988; 1995); Collins (1987; 1991; 1994); Kline (2000); and Thurer (1994).

134 Ruddick, S. 1989. *Maternal Thinking: Toward a Politics of Peace*, p. 111–112.

135 For detailed feminist critique of the role of media and idealized motherhood see, Kaplan, M. 1992. *Motherhood and Representation: The Mother in Popular Culture and Melodrama*. London: Routledge; Kaplan, M. 1993. *Mothers' Images of Motherhood*. New York: Routledge and Douglas, S. and Michaels, M. 2004. *The Mommy Myth: The Idealization of Motherhood and How It Has Undermined All Women*. New York: Free Press.

136 O'Reilly, A. 2006. *Rocking the Cradle: Thoughts on Motherhood, Feminism and the Possibility of Empowered Mothering*. Toronto: Demeter Press, p. 153.

137 O'Reilly, A. 2006. p. 153.

138 A comment made by Shar in the fall of 1996, when she had just celebrated her fiftieth birthday and had recently become a grandmother for the first time.

139 Rich, A. 1986. p. 13.

140 Same-sex couples became legally recognized in Canada on June 20, 2005, with the passing of the Civil Marriage Act.

141 Horwitz, E. 2004. "Resistance As A Site Of Empowerment: The Journey Away From Maternal Sacrifice" in O'Reilly, A. (Ed.). *Mother Outlaws: Theories and Practices of Empowered Mothering*. Toronto: Women's Press, p. 58.

142 See for instance, Green (1999; 204; 2005; 2006, 2008; 2008a, 2009) and O'Reilly, A. 2009a. "Everyday Acts and Heroic Deeds: The Politic, Praxis, and Pedagogy of Feminist Mothering" in Fiona Green, *Feminist Mothering in Theory and Practice: A Study in Transformative Politics*. New York: Edwin Press. i-vi.

143 Spoken by Deb, a 35-year-old heterosexual mother living with her common-law male partner and their biological eight-year-old son, during an interview in 1998.

144 See Gina Wong-Wylie. "Images and Echoes in Matroreform: A Cultural Feminist Perspective." *Journal for the Association for Research on Mothering* 8 (2006):135.

145 Spoken by Deb, a 35-year-old heterosexual mother living with her common-law male partner and their biological eight-year-old son, during an interview in 1998.

146 Green, F. 2009. *Feminist Mothering in Theory and Pracice, 1985–1995*. New York: Edwin Press.

147 For further discussion on the negative influence of the gaze of others on mothers see Sara Ruddick, 1989. *Maternal Thinking: Toward a Politics of Peace*. New York: Ballantine Books, p. 111–112; and Rock, L. 2007. "The 'Good Mother' vs. the 'Other' Mother The Girl Mom." *Journal for the Association for Research on Motherhood* 9(1):20–28.

148 On December 6, 1989, an enraged gunman, Marc Lepine, aged 25, roamed the corridors of Montreal's École Polytechnique for 45 minutes, separated the men from the women, and killed 14 women. Before opening fire on the classroom of female engineering students he screamed, "I hate feminists." Almost immediately, the Montreal Massacre became a galvanizing moment in which mourning turned into outrage about all violence against women. <archives.cbc.ca/society/crime_justice/topics/398/>.

149 The *Employment and Income Assistance Act* made income assistance more contingent on attachment to the paid labour force. The benefit levels were reduced for "employable" individuals and couples without children. People were increasingly expected to participate in training programs or find paid employment. Failure to comply with work expectations could result in a reduction or, in the case of individuals or couples without children, complete loss of income benefits." National Council of Welfare. 1999. *Another Look at Welfare Reform*. Ottawa: National Council of Welfare.

150 See O'Reilly, A. 2008a. "Introduction." In A. O'Reilly (Ed.), *Mother Outlaws: Theories and Practices of Empowered Mothering*. Toronto: Women's Press, p. 11.

151 O'Reilly, A. 2004a. p. 11.

152 See O'Reilly, A. (Ed.). 2004b. "We Were Conspirators, Outlaws From the Institution of Motherhood: Mothering

Against Motherhood for the Possibility of Empowered maternity for Mothers and their Children" in O'Reilly, A. (Ed.), *Mother Outlaws: Theories and Practices of Empowered Mothering*. (59–74). Toronto: Women's Press.

153 See Wong-Wylie, Gina. "Matroreform." *Encyclopedia of Motherhood*. 2010. SAGE Publications; Gina Wong-Wylie.

154 See O'Reilly, A. 2009c. "Maternal Authenticity and the Social Acceptability of Children: Feminist Mothering as Maternal Practice." Philosophical Inquiry into Pregnancy, Childbirth and Mothering Conference. May 14–16. University of Oregon, EMU.

155 O'Brien, L. & Swadender, B. (Eds.). 2006. "Introduction" in O'Brien, L. & Swadender, B. (Eds.), *Writing The Motherline: Mothers, Daughters, And Education*. Lanham, MD: University Press of America, p. xvii.

156 See: Lowinsky, N. 1992. *Stories from the Motherline*. New York: Jeremy P. Tarcher; Lowinsky, N. 2000. "Mothers of Mothers and Daughters: Reflections on the Motherline" in A. O'Reilly & S. Abby (Eds). *Mothers and Daughters: Connection, Empowerment and Transformation*. Maryland: Rowman and Littlefield Publishers, p. 227–235; and Green, F. 2010. "Cultural Bearing" in A. O'Reilly (Ed.). *Encyclopedia of Motherhood, Volume 1*. California, Sage Publications, p. 260–261.

157 O'Reilly, A. 2000. "'I come from a long line of uppity Irate Black Women': African-American Feminist Thought on Motherhood, the Motherline, and Mother-Daughter Relationship" in A. O'Reilly and S. Abby (Eds.) *Mothers and Daughters: Connection, Empowerment and Transformation*. Maryland: Rowman and Littlefield Publishers, p. 143–160.

158 This mother-child relationship is also an important and vital one to the development of transgender children.

159 Green, F. 2010. "Cultural Bearing" in A. O'Reilly (Ed.). *Encyclopedia of Motherhood, Volume 1*. California, Sage Publications, p. 260–261.

160 Green, F. 2010. p. 261.

161 Green, F. 2006. "Developing a Feminist Motherline: Reflections on a Decade of Feminist Parenting." *Journal of the Association for Research on Mothering* Vol. 10 (2):7–20.

162 For further discussion on the ways in which feminist mothers believe they influenced their children see Green, F. "Developing a Feminist Motherline: Reflections on a Decade Feminist Parenting" *Journal for the Association for Research on Mothering* 8 (2006):7–20.

163 Rich, A. 1986. p. 246–7.

164 The original 16 feminist mothers had 35 children, 19 girls and 16 boys. In 2007, all but six girls and nine boys would have been 18 years of age or older. Although the four mothers highlighted in this chapter have a total of 11 children, I was only able to interview five of the nine adult children because of their interest and/or availability.

165 For further discussion, see Chapter 4 in Green's *Feminist Mothering In Theory and Practice, 1985–1995*.

166 See Jane Ursal's *Private Lives, Public Policy* (1992) for further discussion.

167 For further understanding of Beverly's insights, see Green (2009:990–93).

168 According to Maggie Hennessay (2011), the words "womyn" or "wimmin" are used to deliberately set women apart from men. Taking the initiative to rename themselves in this way provides women their own power to be freer and assertive on their own terms. The word "woman" doesn't reflect the fiercely independent nature of feminist movement. Using the term and identifying as a "womyn" makes a political statement of connection with feminist movement.

169 For example, "Between 2000 and 2008, average total income for Canadian women increased at almost twice the pace as it did for men, although women continued to have lower income levels." Statistics Canada. 2008. <www.statcan.gc.ca/daily-quotidien/101216/dq101216c-eng.htm>. According to Statistics Canada, "the percentage of women (15 years of age and over) who participate in the workforce has gone from

45.7% in 1976 to 61.8% in 2005. In 2001, 69.8% of women with children at home (regardless of age) and 65.8% of women with children under two years of age participated in the labour force. Along with the high proportion of women with children who are working, dual-income couples were the majority (61.9% of couples) in 2001. Statistics Canada. 2011. <www4.hrsdc.gc.ca/.3ndic.1t.4r@-eng.jsp?iid=37>.

170 A quote taken from a 1997 interview with Deb, the 35-year-old heterosexual mother of an eight-year-old son.

171 For discussion about the practice and significance of matricide within the Canadian context see Joanna Chiu's article "The Matricide Myth: Does Each New Generation of Feminists Reject its Foremothers?

172 For more information on baby Storm see: Canadian Broadcast Corporation. 2011. CBC Digital Archives. “Parents Of Storm Talk About The Media’s Coverage Of Their Choice To Raise A Sexless Child”; Porter, C. 2011; Poisson, J. 2011. “Parents keep child’s gender secret.” *The Toronto Star*. May 21, 2011. Porter: “The Decision To Raise Baby Storm Without A Gender Stokes Parental Insecurity.” *The Star.com*; Somerville, M. “‘Choice’ for Baby Storm isn’t so simple.” *Ottawa Citizen*. May 28, 2011; Witterick, K. 2011. “Baby Storms Mom On Gender, Parenting And The Media.”

173 For articles on the “slut walk” see: Canadian Broadcasting Corporation. 2011a. “Toronto ‘Slut Walk’ Takes To The Streets.” April 3, 2011; Canadian Broadcasting Corporation. 2011b. “‘Slut Walk’ Hits Saskatoon.” May 28, 2011; Canadian Broadcasting Corporation. 2011c. “Toronto ‘Slut Walk’ Takes To The US.” May 6, 2011.

174 For further information on the Judge Dewar case, see: McIntyre, M. (2011) “Justice Dewar Removed From Cases Of ‘Sexual Nature.’” *Winnipeg Free Press*; Turner, 2011; Canadian Broadcasting Corporation. 2011d. “Manitoba Judge Not Sitting On Criminal Trial.” March 4, 2011; Canadian Broadcasting Corporation. 2011e. “Judge’s Sex Assault Comments Wrong: Professor. No Jail For ‘Clumsy Don Juan.’”

175 *Femministing*. 2011. “A Few Words About Reclaiming ‘Slut.’”

BIBLIOGRAPHY/WORKS CITED

Abbey, S. 1999. Researching Motherhood as a Feminist: Reflecting on My Own Experiences. *Journal of the Association for Research on Mothering*. 1 (1):45–55.

Abbey, S., & O'Reilly, A. 1998. *Redefining Motherhood: Changing Identities and Patterns*. Toronto: Second Story Press.

Adams, A., 1995. Maternal Bonds: Recent Literature on Mothering. *Signs: Journal for Women in Culture and Society*. 20 (2), 414–427.

Ainslie, J., & Feltey, K. 1992. Definitions and Dynamics of Motherhood and Family in Lesbian Communities. *Marriage And Family Review*. 17 (2), 63–85.

Anderson, K. 2000. *A Recognition of Being: Reconstructing Native Womanhood*. Toronto: Second Story Press.

Anderson, K. 2007. "Giving Life to the People: An Indigenous Ideology of Motherhood" in O'Reilly, A. (Ed), *Maternal Theory: Essential Readings*. (761–781). Toronto: Demeter Press.

Apple, R. 1995. Constructing Mothers: Scientific Motherhood in the Nineteenth and Twentieth Centuries. *Social History of Medicine*. (2),161–178.

Apple, R. 2006. *Perfect Motherhood: Science and Childrearing in America*. London: Rutgers University Press.

Arnup, K. 1988. "Lesbian Mothers and Child Custody" in Tigar McLaren, A. (Ed.), *Gender and Society: Creating a Canadian Women's Sociology*. (245–256). Toronto: Copp Clark Pitman.

Arnup, K. 1989. Mothers Just Like Others: Lesbians, Divorce, and Child Custody Canada. *Canadian Journal of Women and the Law* 3 (18)

Arnup, K. 1990. "Educating Mothers: Government Advice for Women in the Inter-War Years" in Arnup, K. et. al. (Eds). (190–210). *Delivering Motherhood: Maternal Ideologies and Practices in the 19th and 20th Centuries.* New York: Routledge.

Arnup, K. 1994. *Education for Motherhood: Advice for Mothers in Twentieth Century Canada.* Toronto: University of Toronto Press.

Arnup, K. (Ed.) 1995. *Lesbian Parenting: Living With Pride and Prejudice.* Charlottetown: Gynergy Books.

Arnup, K., Levesque, A. & Pierson, R. (Eds.) 1990. *Discovering Motherhood: Maternal Ideologies and Practices in the 19th and 20th Centuries.* New York: Routledge.

Badinter, E. 2010. *Le Conflict La Femme et la Mere.* Flammarion: Quebec.

Badinter, E. 1981. *The Myth of Motherhood.* London: Souvenir Press.

Badinter, E. 1986. *The Unopposite Sex: The End of the Gender Battle.* Translated from the French by Barbara Wright. New York: Harper and Row.

Baker, C. L. and Kline, C.B. 1997. *The Conversation Begins: Mothers and Daughters Talk About Living Feminism.* New York: Bantam Dell Pub Group.

Baker, P. 1998. Hearing and Writing Women's Voices. *Resources for Feminist Research.* 26 (112):31–54.

Barrett, M. 1988. *Women's Oppression Today: Problems in Marxist Feminist Analysis.* 2nd Edition. London: Verso.

Barton, A. 2010. Smother Mothers: Give helicopter parents a break. *Globe and Mail. Globe Life.* Sunday, July 25. <www.theglobeandmail.com/life/family-and-relationships/give-helicopter-parents-a-break/article1651532/>. Accessed 7/30/2010.

Bashevkin, S. 1994. Confronting Neo-conservatism: Anglo-American Women's Movements under Thatcher, Reagan and Mulroney. *International Political Science Review.* Vo. 15 (3):275–296.

Begin, M. 1992. "The Royal Commision on the Status of Women in Canada: Twenty Years Later" in Backhouse, C. & Flaherty, D. H. (Eds.), *Changing Times*. (21–38). Montreal: McGill-Queen's University Press.

Belenky, M. F., Clinchy, B. M. and Golderger, N. R. 1986. *Women's Ways of Knowing: The Development of Self, Voice and Mind*. New York: Basic Books.

Bell-Scott, P. and Guy-Sheftall, B. 1991. *Double Stitch: Black Women Writers Write about Mothers and Daughters*. Boston: Beacon Press.

Benjamin, J. 1988. *The Bonds of Love: Psychoanalysis, Feminism and the Problem of Domination*. New York: Pantheon.

Benn, M. 1998. *Madonna and Child: Towards a New Politics of Motherhood*. London: Jonathan Cape.

Bernard, J. 1974. *The Future of Motherhood*. New York: Dial Press.

Bernard, J. 1976. *Women, Wives and Mothers: Values and Options*. Chicago: Aldine.

Blum, L. 1999. *At the Breast: Ideologies of Breast Feeding and Mothering in Contemporary United States*. Boston: Beacon Press.

Boesveld, S. 2009. Mommy Wars: Stay At Home Or Head Back To Work? *Globe and Mail*. June 21. <www.theglobeandmail.com/life/family-and-relationships/mommy-wars/article1191246/>. Accessed 7/26/2010.

Bouvard, M. G. 1994. *Revolutionizing Motherhood: The Mothers of the Plaza de Mayo*. Delaware: Scholarly Books.

Braverman, L. 1989. "Beyond the Myth of Motherhood" in McGoldrick, M., Anderson, C. & Walsh, F. (Eds.), *Women in Families: A Framework for Family Therapy*. (227-243). New York: W.W. Norton & Co.

Buchanan, A. 2003. *Mother Shock: Loving Every (Other) Minute of It*. Berkeley: Seal Press.

Button, L. No date. Helicopter Parents. ParentsCanada.com. <www.parentscanada.com/developing/tweens/articles.aspx?listingid=312>. Accessed 7/30/2010.

Buxton, J. 1998. *Ending the Mother War, Starting the Workplace Revolution*. New York: McMillan.

Canadian Broadcast Corporation. 1989. CBC Digital Archives. <archives.cbc.ca/society/crime_justice/topics/398/>. Accessed 28/01/2011.

Canadian Broadcast Corporation. 2011. CBC Digital Archives. Parents of Storm talk about the media's coverage of their choice to raise a sexless child. <www.cbc.ca/q/episodes/>. Accessed 13/06/2011.

Canadian Broadcasting Corporation. 2011a. Toronto "slut walk" takes to the streets. April 3, 2011. <www.cbc.ca/news/canada/toronto/story/2011/04/03/slut-walk-toronto.html>. Accessed 06/18/2011.

Canadian Broadcasting Corporation. 2011b. "Slut walk" hits Saskatoon. May 28, 2011. <www.cbc.ca/news/canada/saskatchewan/story/2011/05/28/saskatoon-slut-walk-toronto-rape.html>. Accessed 06/18/2011.

Canadian Broadcasting Corporation. 2011c. Toronto "slut walk" takes to the US. May 6, 2011. <www.cbc.ca/news/canada/story/2011/05/06/slut-walk.html>. Accessed 06/18/2011.

Canadian Broadcasting Corporation. 2011d. Manitoba judge not sitting on criminal trial. March 4, 2011. <www.cbc.ca/news/canada/manitoba/story/2011/03/04/mb-deward-jury-trial-not-sitting-110304.html>. Accessed 06/18/2011.

Canadian Broadcasting Corporation. 2011e. Judge's sex assault comments wrong: professor. No jail for "clumsy Don Juan." <www.cbc.ca/news/canada/manitoba/story/2011/02/24/mb-professor-concerns-sex-assault-sentence-manitoba.html>. Accessed 06/18/2011.

Carmichael, C. 1977. *Non Sexist Child Rearing*. Boston: Beacon Press.

Chase, S. and Rogers, M. 2001. *Mothers and Children: Feminist Analysis and Personal Narratives*. New Brunswick, Rutgers.

Chesler, P. 1988. *Sacred Bond: The Legacy of Baby M*. New York: Crown.

Child Care in Canada: An Introduction. <www.mapleleafweb.com/features/child-care-canada-introduction#canadian>.

Chiu, J. 2011. The Matricide Myth: Does Each New Generation of Feminists Reject its Foremothers? *Herizons: Women's News and Feminist Views*. 25 (2): 16–19.

Chodorow, N. 1978. *The Reproduction of Mothering: Psychoanalysis and Sociology of Gender*. Berkley: University of California Press.

Chodorow, N. and Contratto, S.. 1982. "The Fantasy of the Perfect Mother" in Thorne, B. and Yalome, M. (Eds.), *Rethinking the Family: Some Feminist Questions*. (54–71). New York: Longman.

Chua, A. 2011. *Battle Hymn of the Tiger Mother*. New York: Penguin.

Cixous, H. 1986. *The Newly Born Woman*. Minneapolis: The University of Minnesota Press.

Coll, C., Surrey, J. & Weingarten, K. (Eds.). 1998. *Mothering Against the Odds: Diverse Voices of Contemporary Mothers*. New York: Guildford Press.

Code, L. 1991. *What Can She Know? Feminist Theory and the Construction of Knowledge*. Ithaca, New York: Cornell University Press.

Collins, P. H. 1987. The Meaning of Motherhood in Black Culture and Black Mother/Daughter Relationships. *Sage: A Scholarly Journal on Black Women*. 1 (2):3–10

Collins, P. H. 1989. The Social Construction of Black Feminist Thought. *Signs Journal for Women in Culture and Society*. 14 (41):745–773.

Collins, P. H. 1991;2000. *Black Feminist Thought: Knowledge, Consciousness and the Politics of Empowerment*. New York: Routledge.

Collins, P. H. 1994. "Shifting the Centre: Race, Class, and Feminist Theorizing about Motherhood" in Nakano, E., Chang, G. & Forcey, L. (Eds.), *Mothering: Ideology, Experience, and Agency*. (45–66). New York: Routledge.

Corrin, C. 1994. "Fighting Back or Biting back? Lesbian's in Higher Education" in Davis, S., Lubelska, C., & Quinn, J. (Eds.), *Changing the Subject: Women in Higher Education.* (58–74). London: Taylor & Francis.

Crawford, S. 1987. "Lesbian Families: Psychological Stress and the Family-Building Process" in Boston Lesbian Psychologies Collective (Ed.), *Lesbian Psychologies: Explorations and Challenges.* (195–214). Chicago: University of Illinois Press.

Crittenden, A. 2002. *The Price of Motherhood: Why the Most Important Job in the World is Still the Least Valued.* New York: Holt Paperbacks.

Dally, A. 1982. *Inventing motherhood: The Consequence of an Ideal.* London: Burnett Books.

Davies, B. and Welch, D. 1986. Motherhood and Feminism: Are They Compatible? The Ambivalence of Mothering. *Australian and New Zealand Journal of Sociology.* 22 (3):411–426.

Davin, A. 1978. Imperialism and Motherhood. *History Workshop.* 5, 9–65.

de Beauvoir, S. 1949. *The Second Sex.* Translated by H M Parshley, Penguin 1972.

Demeter Press <www.yorku.ca/arm/demeterpress.html>. Accessed 2/28/10.

DiLipi, E. M. 1989. Lesbian Mothers and the Motherhood Hierarchy. *Journal of Homosexuality.* 18(1–2):101–21.

Dill, B. T. 1988. Our Mother's Grief: Racial Ethnic Women and the Maintenance of Families. *Journal of Family History.* Vol. 13:415–431.

Dinnerstein, D. 1976. *The Mermaid and the Minotaur: Sexual Arrangements and Human Malaise.* New York: Harper and Row.

Dixon, P. 1991. *Mothers and Mothering: An Annotated Feminist Bibliography.* New York: Garland Publishing.

Douglas, S. and Michaels, M. 2004. *The Mommy Myth: The Idealization of Motherhood and How It Has Undermined All Women.* New York: Free Press.

Driver, S. & Newman Z. 2011. *Queer Parenting*. Toronto, Demeter Press.

DuPlessis, R. (Ed). 1978. Special Issue on Motherhood. *Feminist Studies*. Vol. 4 (2).

Eisenstein, H. 1983. "The Cultural Meaning of Mothering: As Experience and Institution" in Eisenstein, H. (Ed.), *Contemporary Feminist Thought*. (69–78). Boston: G.K. Hall.

Epstein, R. (Ed.) 2010. *Who's Your Daddy?And Other Writings on Queer Parenting*. Toronto: Sumach Press.

Eyer, D. 1996. *Motherguilt: How our Culture Blames Mothers for What's Wrong with Society*. New York: Times Books Random House.

Faludi, S. 2010. American Electra: Feminism's ritual matricide. *Harper's Magazine*. October: 29–42.

Faludi, S. 1991. *Backlash: The Undeclared War Against American Women*. New York: Crown.

Femministing. 2011. A few words about reclaiming "slut." <feministing.com/2011/05/16/a-few-words-about-reclaiming-%E2%80%9Cslut%E2%80%9D/>. Accessed 06/18/2011.

Ferguson, A. 1989. *Blood at the Root: Motherhood, Sexuality and Male Dominance*. London: Pandora.

Firestone, S. 1970. *The Dialectic of Sex: The Case for Feminist Revolution*. New York: Marrow.

Flax, J. 1978. The Conflict Between Nurturance and Autonomy within Mother/Daughter Relations and Within Feminism. *Feminist Studies*. Vol 4 (2):171–189.

Fonow, M. & Cook, J. 1991. "Back to the Future: A Look at the Second Wave of Feminist Epistemology and Methodology" in Fonow, M. & Cook, J. (Eds.), *Beyond Methodology: Feminist Scholarship as Lived Research*. (1–15). Indianapolis: Indiana University Press.

Forcey, L. R. 1999. "Book Review." *Signs*. Vol. 25(1):301.

Forna, A. 1999. *Mother of All Myths: How Society Moulds and Constrains Mothers*. London: Harper Collins.

Freely, M. 1995. *What About Us? An Open Letters to the Mothers Feminism Forgot*. London: Bloomsberg.

French, M. 1977. *The Women's Room*. New York: Summit Books.

Friedan, B. 1963. *The Feminine Mystique*. New York: W.W. Norton.

Friedan, B. 1981. *The Second Stage*. New York: Summit Books.

Friedman, M. & Shana Calixte S. (Eds.) 2009. *Mothering and Blogging*. Toronto, Demeter Press.

Friedman, R. 2010. When Bad Eggs Happen To Good Parents: When A Child's Misbehaviour Is Chronic, We Tend To Blame Mom And Dad, But Even The Best Nest Can Produce Toxic Offspring. *The Globe and Mail*. July, 16. L5.

Gibbs, N. 2009. The Growing Backlash Against Overparenting. *Time*. Friday, November 20. <www.time.com/time/nation/article/0,8599,1940395,00.html>. Accessed 7/26/2010.

Gieve, K. 1987. Rethinking Feminist Attitudes Towards Motherhood. *Feminist Review*. 25, 38–45.

Gilligan, C. 1982. *In a Different Voice: Psychological Theory and Women's Development*. Massachusetts: Harvard University Press.

Girls Gone Child. <www.girlsgonechild.net>. Accessed 06/18/2011.

Glaser, B. 1978. *Theoretical Sensitivity: Advances in the Methodology of Grounded Theory*. Mill Valley, Ca: Sociology Press.

Glaser, B. 1992. *Basics of Grounded Theory Analysis: Emergence vs. Forcing*. Mill Valley, Ca.: Sociology Press.

Glaser, B. 1998. *Doing Grounded Theory: Issues and Discussions*. Mill Valley, Ca.: Sociology Press.

Glaser, B., & Strauss, A. 1967. *The Discovery of Grounded Theory: Strategies for Qualitative Research*. Chicago: Aldine Publishing Co.

Glenn, E. 1994. "Social Constructions of Mothering: A Thematic Overview" in Glen, E., Chang, G. & Forcey, L. (Eds.), *Mothering: Ideology, Experience, and Agency*. (1–29) New York: Routledge.

Glenn, E., Chang, G. & Forcey, L. (Eds.). 1994. *Mothering: Ideology, Experience, and Agency*. New York: Routledge.

Glickman, R. 1993. *Daughters of Feminists*. New York: St. Martin's Press.

Gordon, T. 1990. *Feminist Mothers*. New York: New York University Press.

Gore, A. 1998. *Hip Mama Survival Guide, The: Advice From the Trenches On: Pregnancy, Childbirth, Cool Names, Clueless Doctors*. New York: Hyperion.

Gore, A. 2000. *The Mother Trip: Hip Mama's Guide to Staying Sane in the Chaos of Motherhood*. Berkeley: Seal Press.

Gore, A. and Lavender, B. (Eds.). 2001. *Breeder: Real-Life Stories from the New Generation of Mothers*. Berkeley: Seal Press.

Gore, J. 1992. "What We Can Do for You! What Can 'We' Do for 'You'?" in Luke, C. & J. Gore (Eds.), *Feminisms and Critical Pedagogy*. (54–73). New York: Routledge.

Green, F. 1999. Living Feminism Through Mothering. *Journal for the Association of Research on Mothering*. 1 (1):99–104

Green, F. 2003. What's Love Got To Do With It? A Personal Reflection on the Role of Maternal Love in Feminist Teaching. *Journal of the Association for Research on Mothering*. 5 (2): 47–56.

Green, F. 2004. "Feminist Mothers: Successfully Negotiating the Tension Between Motherhood as 'Institution' and 'Experience'" in O'Reilly, A. (Ed.), *From Motherhood to Mothering The Legacy of Adrienne Rich's Of Woman Born*. (161–176) Albany, SUNY.

Green, F. 2005. Feminist Mothering: Challenging Gender Inequality by Resisting the Institution of Motherhood and Raising Children to be Critical Agents of Social Change. *Socialist Studies* 1 (1):83–99.

Green, F. 2006. Developing a Feminist Motherline: Reflections on a Decade of Feminist Parenting. *Journal of the Association for Research on Mothering*. 8 (2): 17–20.

Green, F. 2008. "Feminist Motherline: Embodied Knowledge/s of Feminist Mothering" in O'Reilly, A. (Ed.), *Feminist Mothering*. (161–176). Albany: SUNY.

Green, F. 2008a. Matroreform: Feminist Mothers and Their Daughters Creating Feminist Motherlines. *Journal for the Association for Research on Mothering*. 10 (2):11–21.

Green, F. 2009. *Feminist Mother in Theory and Practice, 1985–1995*. New York: Mellen Press.

Green, F. 2010. "Association for Research on Mothering" in O'Reilly, A. & Golsen, G. (Eds.), *Encyclopedia on Motherhood*. 85–86. Sage Press.

Green, F. 2010. "Cultural Bearing" in O'Reilly, A. & Golsen, G. (Eds.), *Encyclopedia on Motherhood*. 260–261. Sage Press.

Green, F. 2010. "Demeter Press" in O'Reilly, A. (Ed.), *Encyclopedia on Motherhood*. 279. Sage Press.

Green, F. 2010. "Patriarchal Ideology of Motherhood" in O'Reilly, A. (Ed.), *Encyclopedia on Motherhood*. 969–970. Sage Press.

Green, F. 2011. Feminist Maternal Pedagogies: Inside and Outside the Classroom in D. Byrd and F. Green (Eds.), *Maternal Pedagogies: In and Outside the Classroom*. Toronto: Demeter Press, 197-211.

Griffin, K. & Molhalland, L.A. (Eds.). 1997 *Lesbian Motherhood in Europe*. London: Cassell.

Grupo Feminista Miercoles. 1980. Recreating Motherhood: The Concept of Motherhood as an Instrument of Ideological Domination. *Herizons* 1 (1):28.

Hallstein, L. & O'Brien, D. 2008. "Second Wave Silences and Third Wave Intensive Mothering" in Kinser, A. (Ed.), *Mothering in the Third Wave*. (107–118) Toronto: Demeter Press.

Hamilton, R. 1990. Feminism and Motherhood, 1970–1990: Reinventing the Wheel? *RFR/DRF*, 19 (3/4), 23–31.

Harcourt, W. 2006. *Feminist Praxis: Women's Transnational and Place Based Struggles for Change*. Great Transition Initiative Paper Series, Frontiers of a Great Change 11. Boston: Tellus Institute for a Great Transition.

Harding, S. 1987. "Introduction" in Harding, S. (Ed.), *Feminism and Methodology Social Science Issues*. (1–14). Milton Keynes: Open University Press.

Hays, S. 1996. *The Cultural Contradictions of Motherhood*. New Haven: Yale University Press.

Hays, S. 2010. *The Cultural Contradictions of Motherhood.* Yale University Press. <yalepress.yale.edu/yupbooks/book.asp?isbn=9780300066821>. Accessed 7/31/2010.

Hennessey, M. 2011. My Eyes Are Up Here: That's Womyn With A "Y" If You Please. *The Pioneer Log*. Thursday, January 27, 2011 at 04:31 AM <www.piolog.com/opinion/2011/1/27/my-eyes-are-up-here-thats-womyn-with-a-y-if-you-please.html>. Accessed 11/3/18.

Hernandex, D. & Rehman, B. (Eds). 2002. *Colonize This! Young Women of Color on Today's Feminism.* New York: Seal.

Hewlett, S. 1986. *A Lesser Life: The Myth of Women's Liberation in America.* New York: William Morrow & Co.

Heywood, A. 2003. *Political Ideologies: An Introduction.* Palgrave Macmillan.

Hill, M. 1987. "Child-Rearing Attitudes of Black Lesbian Mothers" in Boston Lesbian Psychologies Collective (Ed.), *Lesbian Psychologies: Explorations and Challenges.* (215–226). Chicago: University of Illinois Press.

Hirsch, M. 1981. Mothers and Daughters. *Signs.* Vol. 7 (1):203.

Hirsch, M. 1989. *The Mother/Daughter Plot: Narrative, Psychoanalysis, Feminism.* Bloomington: Indiana University Press.

Hirsch, M. 1997. "Feminism at the Maternal Divide: A Diary" in Jetter, A. Orleck A., & Taylor, D. (Eds.), *The Politics of Motherhood: Activist Voices from Left to Right.* Hanover: University Press of New England.

Hoffnung, M. 1989. "Motherhood: Contemporary Conflict for Women" in Freeman, J. (Ed.), *Women: A Feminist Perspective.* (157–175). Fourth Edition. California: Mayfield.

hooks, b. 1981. *Ain't I a Woman: Black Women and Feminism.* Boston: South End Press.

hooks, b. 1984. *Feminist Theory: From Margin to Center.* Boston: South End Press.

hooks, b. 1988. *Talking Back: Thinking Feminist, Thinking Black.* Toronto: Between the Lines.

hooks, b. 2000. *Feminism is for Everybody: Passionate Politics*. New York: South End Press.

Hochschild, A. 1989. *The Second Shift Working Parents and the Revolution at Home*. New York: Viking.

Horwitz , E. 2011. *Through the Maze of Motherhood Empowered Mothers Speak* Toronto: Demeter Press.

Horwitz, E. 2004. "Resistance As A Site Of Empowerment: The Journey Away From Maternal Sacrifice" in O'Reilly, A. (Ed.), *Mother Outlaws: Theories and Practices of Empowered Mothering. (43–57)*. Toronto: Women's Press.

Hulbert, A. 2003. *Raising America: Experts, Parents, and a Century of Advice About Children*. New York: Alfred A. Knopf.

Irigaray, L. (1981) And the One Doesn't Stir Without the Other. *Signs*. Vol 7 (1) :60–67.

Irigaray, L. (1985) *This Sex Which is Not One*. New York: Cornell University Press.

Jagger, B. 2009. In *Ethics and International Affairs: A Reader* by Roesenthal, J.H. and Barry, C. (Eds.), 3rd Edition.

Johnston, D. & Swanson, D. 2003. Invisible Mothers: A Content Analysis of Motherhood Ideologies and Myths in Magazines. *Sex Roles*. Vol. 49 (1/2):21–33

Kadi, J.1994. *Food for Our Grandmothers: Writings by Arab-American and Arab-Canadian Feminists*. New York: South End Press.

Kaplan, A. 1992. *Motherhood And Representation: The Mother In Popular Culture And Melodrama*. London: Routledge.

Kaplan, M. 1993. *Mothers' Images of Motherhood*. New York: Routledge.

Keller, K. 2000. *Disciplining Young Children*. Minnesota, Capstone Press

Kinser, A. (Ed.). 2010. *Motherhood and Feminism*. Seal Press.

Kinser, A. 2010a. "Introduction" in Kinser, A. (Ed.), *Mothering in the Third Wave*. Toronto: Demeter Press.

Kinser, A. (Ed.). 2008. *Mothering in the Third Wave*. Toronto, Demeter Press.

Kinser, A. 2008a. "Mothering as Relational Consciousness" in O'Reilly, A. (Ed.), *Feminist Mothering* (123–140). Toronto: Demeter Press.

Kirby, S. & McKenna, K. 1989. *Experience, Research, Social Change: Methods from the Margins*. Toronto: Garamond Press.

Kirby, S., Greaves, L. and Reid, C. 2006. *Experience, Research, Social Change: Methods Beyond the Mainstream*. Peterborough, ON: Broadview Press

Kline, M. 2000. "Complicating the Ideology of Motherhood: Child Welfare Law and First Nation Women" in Crow, B. & Gotell, L. (Eds.), *Open Boundaries: A Canadian Women's Studies Reader*. (194–204). Toronto: Prentice Hall.

Knowles, J. P. & Cole, E. (Eds.) 1990. *Woman-Defined Motherhood*. (1–7). New York: Harrington Park Press.

Kuperberg, A. & Stone, P. 2008. The Media Depiction of Women Who Opt Out. *Gender and Society*. Vol. 22(4):497–517.

Kuttai, H. 2010. *Maternity Rolls: Pregnancy, Childbirth and Disability*. Halifax and Winnipeg: Fernwood Publishing.

Ladd-Taylor, M. and Umansky, L. (Eds.). 1998. *"Bad" Mothers: The Politics of Blame in Twentieth-Century America*. New York: New York University Press.

Latchford, F. (Ed.) 2010. *Adoption and Mothering*. Toronto, Demeter Press.

Latina Mami <lagloria.typepad.com/latinamami>. Accessed 2/28/10.

Lavell, J. and Lavell-Harvard, D. 2006. *Until Our Hearts Are On the Ground: Aboriginal Mothering, Oppression, Resistance and Rebirth*. Toronto, Demeter Press.

Lazarre, J. 1976; 1997. *The Mother Knot*. Durham: Duke University Press.

Lewin, E. 1994. "Negotiating Lesbian Motherhood: The Dialectics of Resistance and Accommodation" in Glen, E., Chang, G. & Forcey, L. (Eds.), *Mothering: Ideology, Experience, and Agency*. (237–258). New York: Routledge.

Lewis, D. S., & Yoest, C.C. 1996. *Mother in the Middle: Searching for Peace in the Mommy Wars*. Grand Rapids, MI: Zondervan.

Lewis, J. 1990. "'Motherhood Issues' in the Late Nineteenth and Twentieth Centuries" in Arnup, K. et. al. (Eds.), (1–19). *Delivering Motherhood: Maternal Ideologies and Practices in the 19th and 20th Centuries*. New York: Routledge.

Literary Mama <www.literarymama.com>. Accessed 2/28/10.

Lorde, A. 1987. "Turning the Beat Around: Lesbian Parenting" in Pollack, S. & Vaughn, J. (Eds.), *Politics of the Heart: A Lesbian Parenting Anthology*. (310–324). New York: Firebrand Books.

Lowinsky, N. 1992. *Stories from the Motherline*. New York: Jeremy P. Tarcher.

Lowinsky, N. 2000. "Mothers of Mothers and Daughters: Reflections on the Motherline" in O'Reilly, A. & Abby, S. (Eds). *Mothers and Daughters: Connection, Empowerment and Transformation*. (227–235). Maryland: Rowman and Littlefield Publishers.

Mack-Canty, C. & Wright, S. 2008. "Parenting in Third Wave Feminism and Empowering All Family Members" in O'Reilly, A. (Ed.), *Feminist Mothering*. (143–159). Albany: SUNY.

Maroney, H. J. 1985. Embracing Motherhood: New Feminist Theory. *Canadian Journal of Political and Social Theory*. 9 (1), 40–64.

McIntyre, M. (2011) Justice Dewar Removed From Cases Of "Sexual Nature." *Winnipeg Free Press*.

Maushart, S. 2000. *The Mask of Motherhood: How Becoming a Mother Changes Our Lives and Why We Never Talk About It*. New York: Penguin.

Mohanty, C. 2003. *Feminism without Borders: Decolonizing Theory, Practicing Solidarity*. Duke University Press.

Mohanty, C. 1991. "Introduction" in Mohanty, Russo, Torres (Eds.), *Third World Women and the Politics of Feminism*. Bloomington and Indianapolis: Indiana University Press.

Mohanty, C. 1991a. "Under Western Eyes" in Mohanty, C., Russo, A., and Torres, L. (Eds.). *Third World Women and the Politics of Feminism*. Bloomington and Indianapolis: Indiana University Press.

Moraga, C. & Anzaldue, M. (Eds.) 1981. *This Bridge Called My Back: Writings by Radical Women of Color*. New York: Kitchen Table: Women of Color Press.

Morgan, R. 1978. *Going Too Far: The Personal Chronicle of a Feminist*. New York: Vintage.

Morrison, T. 1987. *Beloved*. New York: Penguin Books.

Morrison, T. 1973. *Sula*. New York: Penguin Books.

Mothers Acting Up <www.mothersactingup.org>.

Mothers & More <www.mothersandmore.org>.

Mothers Are Women <www.mothersarewomen.com>.

Mullins, A. 2005. *Reconceiving Pregnancy and Childcare: Ethics, Experience, and Reproductive Labor*. Cambridge: Cambridge University Press.

Museum of Motherhood <www.museumofmotherhood.org/Info.html>.

National Council of Welfare. 1999. *Another Look at Welfare Reform*. Ottawa: National Council of Welfare.

Nelson, F. 1996. *Lesbian Motherhood: An Exploration of Canadian Lesbian Families*. Toronto: Toronto University. Press.

North American Aerospace Defense Command. <www.norad.mil/about/index.html>. Accessed 6/09/2011.

Notes From the Trenches. <www.notesfromthetrenches.com>. Accessed 7/06/10.

Oakley, A. 1986. "Feminism, Motherhood and Medicine—Who Cares?" in Mitchell, J. & Oakley, A. (Eds.), *What is Feminism?* (127–150). New York: Pantheon.

O'Brien, M. 1981. *The Politics of Reproduction*. London: Routledge & Kegan Paul.

O'Brien, L. & Swadender, B. (Eds.) 2006. "Introduction" in O'Brien, L. & Swadender, B. (Eds.), *Writing The Motherline: Mothers, Daughters, And Education*. (i-xvii) Lanham, MD: University Press of America.

Okin, S. 1989. *Justice, Gender and the Family*. New York: Basic Books.

O'Reilly, A. 2000. "'I Come From A Long Line Of Uppity Irate Black Women': African-American Feminist Thought on Motherhood, the Motherline, and Mother-Daughter Relationship" in O'Reilly, A. and S. Abby (Eds.), *Mothers and Daughters: Connection, Empowerment and Transformation*. (143–160). Maryland: Rowman and Littlefield Publishers.

O'Reilly, A. 2004. *From Motherhood to Mothering: The Legacy of Adrienne Rich's Of Woman Born*. Toronto: Demeter Press.

O'Reilly, A. (Ed.) 2001a. *Mothers and Sons: Feminism, Masculinity and the Struggle to Raise our Sons*. New York: Routledge Press.

O'Reilly, A. 2004. *Toni Morrison and Motherhood: A Politics of the Heart*. Albany: SUNY.

O'Reilly, A. (Ed.) 2004a. "Introduction" in O'Reilly, A. (Ed.), *Mother Outlaws: Theories and Practices of Empowered Mothering*. Toronto: Women's Press.

O'Reilly, A. 2004b. "'We Were Conspirators, Outlaws from the Institution of Motherhood': Mothering against Motherhood and the Possibility of Empowered Maternity for Mothers and Their Children" in O'Reilly, A. (Ed.), *Mother Outlaws: Theories and Practices of Empowered Mothering*. (59–73). Toronto: Women's Press.

O'Reilly, A. (Ed.) 2004c. *From Motherhood to Mothering: The Legacy of Adrienne Rich's Of Woman Born*, Albany: SUNY.

O'Reilly, A. 2006. *Rocking the Cradle: Thoughts on Motherhood, Feminism, and the Possibility of Empowered Mothering*. Toronto: Demeter Press.

O'Reilly, A. (Ed.) 2007. *Maternal Theory: Essential Readings*. Toronto: Demeter Press.

O'Reilly, A. (Ed.) 2008. *Feminist Mothering*. Albany: SUNY.

O'Reilly, A. 2008a. "Introduction" in O'Reilly, A. (Ed.), *Feminist Mothering*. (1–24). Albany: SUNY.

O'Reilly, A. 2009. "Introduction" in O'Reilly, A. (Ed.), *Maternal Thinking: Philosophy, Politics, Practice*. (1–13). Toronto: Demeter Press.

O'Reilly, A. 2009a. "Everyday Acts and Heroic Deeds: The Politic, Praxis and Pedagogy of Feminist Mothering" in Green, F. *Feminist Mothering in Theory and Practice: A Study in Transformative Politics*. New York: Edwin Press. i-vi.

O'Reilly, A. (Ed.) 2009b. *Motherhood at the 21st Century: Policy, Identity, Experience and Agency*. New York: Columbia University Press.

O'Reilly, A. 2009c. "Maternal Authenticity and the Social Acceptability of Children: Feminist Mothering as Maternal Practice." Philosophical Inquiry into Pregnancy, Childbirth and Mothering Conference. May 14–16. University of Oregon, EMU.

O'Reilly, A. (Ed.) 2010. *Encyclopedia of Mothering*. New York: Sage Press.

O'Reilly, A. (Ed.) 2011. *The 21st Century Movement: Mothers Speak Out on Why We Need to Change the World and How to Do It*. Toronto: Demeter Press.

O'Reilly, A. & Abbey, S. (Eds.). 2000. *Mothers and Daughters: Connection, Empowerment and Transformation*, New York: Rowman and Littlefield.

O'Reilly, A., Porter, M. and Short, P. (Eds.). 2001. *Motherhood: Power and Oppression*, Toronto: Women's Press.

O'Reilly, A and Ruddick, S. 2009. "A Conversation about Maternal Thinking" in O'Reilly, A. (Ed.), *Maternal Thinking: Philosophy, Politics, Practice*. Toronto: Demeter Press. 14–38.

Off Our Backs Collective. 2006. Feminism and Motherhood Issues. *Off Our Backs*. Vol. 36(1).

Orleck, A. 1997. "Tradition Unbound: Radical Mothers in International Perspective" in Jettner, A., Orleck, A. and Taylor, D. (Eds.), *The Politics of Motherhood: Activist Voices from Left to Right*. (3–22).Hanover: University Press of New England.

Peskowitz, M. 2005. *The Truth Behind the Mommy Wars: Who Decides What Makes a Good Mother?* New York: Seal Press.

Pharr, S. 1997. *Homophobia: A Weapon of Sexism*. Expanded Edition. Arizona: Chardon Press.

Phoenix, A. & Woollett, A. 1991. "Motherhood: Social construction, politics and psychology" in Phoenix, A. Woollett, A. & Lloyd, E. (Eds.), *Motherhood: Meanings, Practices and Ideologies*. (13–27). London: Sage.

Poisson, J. 2011. Parents Keep Child's Gender Secret. *The Toronto Star*. May 21, 2011. <www.thestar.com/article/995112>. Accessed 06/19/2011.

Polikoff, N. 1987. "Lesbians Choosing Children: The Personal is Political Revisited" in Pollack, S. & Vaughn, J. (Eds.), *Politics of the Heart: A Lesbian Parenting Anthology*. (48–54). New York: Firebrand Books.

Pollack, S. 1987. "Lesbian Mothers: A Lesbian-Feminist Perspective on Research" in Pollack, S. & Vaughn, J. (Eds.), *Politics of the Heart: A Lesbian Parenting Anthology*. (316–324). New York: Firebrand Books.

Pollack, S. 1990. "Lesbian Parents: Claiming Our Visibility" in Knowles, J. & Cole, E. (Eds.), *Woman-Defined Motherhood*. (181–194). London: Hawarth Press.

Pollack, S. & Vaughn, J. (Eds.), *Politics of the Heart: A Lesbian Parenting Anthology*. New York: Firebrand Books.

Porter, C. 2011. Porter: The decision to raise baby Storm without a gender stokes parental insecurity. *The Star.com*. May 27, 2011. <www.thestar.com/article/998689--porter-the-decision-to-raise-baby-storm-without-a-gender-stokes-parental-insecurity>. Accessed 06/18/2011.

Rebick. J. 2005. *Ten Thousand Roses: The Making of a Feminist Revolution*. Toronto: Penguin.

Reddy, M. T. 1994. "Race-ing Love" in Reddy, M., Roth, M. & Sheldon, A. (Eds.), *Mother Journeys: Feminists Write About Mothering*. (85–92). Minneapolis: Spinsters Ink.

Reddy, M. T., Roth, M., & Sheldon, A. (Eds.) 1994. *Mother Journeys: Feminists Write About Mothering*. Minneapolis: Spinsters Ink.

Reinharz, S. 1992. *Feminist Methods in Social Research*. Oxford: Oxford University Press.

Rich, A. 1976 [1986]. *Of Woman Born: Motherhood as Experience and Institution*. London: Virago.

Richardson, D. 1993. *Women, Motherhood and Child Rearing*. London: Macmillian.

Rock, L. 2007. The "Good Mother" vs. the "Other" Mother The Girl Mom. *Journal for the Association for Research on Motherhood* 9(1):20–28

Rothman, B. K. 1989. *Recreating Motherhood: Ideology and Technology in a Patriarchal Society*. New York: W. W. Norton & Company.

Rothman, B. K. 1994. "Beyond Mothers and Fathers: Ideology in a Patriarchal Society" in Glenn, N. et. al. (Eds.), *Mothering: Ideology, Experience, and Agency*. (139–157). New York: Routledge.

Ruddick, S. 1980. Maternal Thinking. *Feminist Studies*. Vol. 6 (2): 342–367.

Ruddick, S. 1983. "Maternal Thinking" in Trebilcot, J. (Ed.), *Mothering: Essays in Feminist Theory*. (213–230). New Jersey: Rowman and Allanheld.

Ruddick, S. 1989;1995. *Maternal Thinking: Toward a Politics of Peace*. Boston: Beacon Press.

Sangster, J. 1995. "Doing Two Jobs: The Wage-Earning Mother, 1945–70" in Parr, J. (Ed.), *A Diversity of Women: Ontario, 1945–1980*. pp. 98–134. Toronto: University of Toronto Press.

Scarth, F. 2004. *The Other Within: Ethics, Politics and the Body in Simone de Beauvoir*. Lanham and Oxford: Rowman & Littlefield.

Schutze, Y. 1987. The Good Mother: The History of the Normative Model "Mother-Love." *Sociological Studies of Child Development*. 2: 39–78.

Smith, A. 2001. Mass-market Magazine Portrayals of Working Mothers and other Related Issues, 1987 and 1997. *Journal of Children and Poverty*. Vol. 7:101–119.

Smith, D. 1990. "Women's Work as Mothers: A New Look at the Relation of Class, Family and School Achievement" in Forman, F., O'Brien, M., Haddad, J., Hallman, D. & Masters, P. (Eds.), *Feminism and Education: A Canadian Perspective*. (219–244). Toronto: Centre for Women's Studies in Education Ontario Institute for Studies in Education.

Somerville, M. "Choice" for Baby Storm isn't so simple. *Ottawa Citizen*. May 28, 2011. <www.ottawacitizen.com/Choice+Baby+Storm+simple/4847012/story.html#ixzz1Pg12T2s>. Accessed 06/18/2011.

Snitow, A. 1992. Feminism and Motherhood: An American Reading. *Feminist Review*. Vo. 40: 32–51.

Spivak, G. C. 1996. *The Spivak Reader*. Eds. D. Landry and G. MacLean. Great Britain: Routledge.

Stanley, L. 1990. *Feminist Praxis: Research, Theory and Epistemology in Feminist Sociology*. New York: Routledge.

Stacey, J. 1993. Untangling Feminist Theory. In D. Richardson & V. Robinson (Eds.), *Thinking Feminist: Key Concepts in Women's Studies*. (49–73). New York: Guilford Press.

Stanley, L., & Wise, S. 1993. *Breaking Out Again: Feminist Ontology and Epistemology*. London: Routledge.

Statistics Canada. 2000. *Women in Canada: A Gender Based Statistical Report*. Catalogue No. 89–503-XPE.

Statistics Canada. 2006. Census snapshot of Canada — Families. <www.statcan.gc.ca/pub/11-008-x/2007006/article/10380-eng.htm>. Accessed 12/5/2010.

Statistics Canada. 2006a. Mother's Day… By the numbers. <www42.statcan.ca/smr08/2006/smr08_047_2006-eng.htm>. Accessed 12/6/10.

Statistics Canada. 2008. Women in Canada: Economic well-being. <www.statcan.gc.ca/daily-quotidien/101216/dq101216c-eng.htm>. Accessed 3/31/2011.

Statistics Canada. 2011. Indicators of Well-being in Canada: Canadians in Context — Households and Families. Human Resources and Skills Development Canada. <www4.hrsdc.gc.ca/.3ndic.1t.4r@-eng.jsp?iid=37>. Accessed 4/01/2011.

Steiner, L. M. 2007. *Mommy Wars: Stay-at-Home and Career Moms Face Off on Their Choices, Their Lives, Their Families*. New York: Random House.

Strauss, A. & Corbin, J. 1990. *The Basics of Qualitative Research: Grounded Theory Procedures and Techniques*. London: Sage.

Strauss, A. & Corbin, J. 1994. "Grounded Theory Methodology: An Overview" in Norman, D. & Lincoln, Y. (Eds.), *Handbook of Qualitative Research*. (273–285). London: Sage Publications.

Strauss, A. & Corbin, J. 1997. *Grounded Theory in Practice*. Thousand Oakes, CA: Sage.

Strauss, A. & Corbin, J. 2007. *Basics of Qualitative Research Techniques and Procedures for Developing Grounded Theory*. Third Edition. Thousand Oakes, CA: Sage

Strong, M. S., and Rowe-Finkbeiner, K. 2008. *The Maternal is Political: Women Writers at the Intersection of Motherhood and Social Change*. New York: Seal Press.

Strong-Boag, V. 1976. *The Parliament of Women: The National Council of Women of Canada 1893-1929*. Ottawa: National Museum of Man.

Sydie, R. A. 1994. *Natural Women, Cultured Men: A Feminist Perspective on Sociological Theory*. Vancouver: University of British Columbia Press.

Taylor, D. 1997. "Overview: The Uneasy Relationship between Motherhood and Feminism" in Jettner, A., Orleck, A. and Taylor, D. (Eds.), *The Politics of Motherhood: Activist Voices from Left to Right*. (349–351). Hanover: University Press of New England.

The Daily Reporter. 2011. Are these the most PC parents in the world? The couple raising a "genderless baby"... to protect his (or her) right to choice. Mailonline. <www.dailymail.co.uk/news/article-1389593/Kathy-Witterick-David-Stocker-raising-genderless-baby.html>.

The Mothers Movement Online, <www.mothersmovement.org>. Accessed 2/28/10.

Thurer, S. 1994. *The Myths of Motherhood: How Culture Reinvents the Good Mother*. New York: Penguin.

Trebilcot, J. (Ed.) 1983. *Mothering: Essays in Feminist Theory*. New Jersey: Rowman and Allanheld.

Trinh, Minh-ha. 1989. Difference: A Special Third World Woman Issue. *Discourse* 8 (86–87):10–37.

Tucker, J. Stadtman 2006. "Care as a Cause: Framing the Twenty-First-Century Mother's Movement" in Hamington, M. and Miller, D. (Eds.), *Socializing Care: Feminist Ethics and Public Issues*. (183–203). New York: Rowman & Littlefield Publishers.

Turnbull, L. 2001. *Double Jeopardy: Motherwork and the Law*. Toronto: Sumach Press.

Turner, J. 2011. Appeal court reviewing Dewar decision. March 2, 2011. <www.cbc.ca/news/canada/manitoba/story/2011/03/02/mb-dewar-sexual-assault-case-review-winnipeg.html>.

Udel, L. 2001. Revision and Resistance: The Politics of Native Women's Motherwork. *Frontiers: A Journal of Women Studies 22.2: 43–62*.

Umansky, L. 1996. *Motherhood Reconceived: Feminism and the Legacies of the Sixties*. New York: New York University Press.

Ursel, J. 1992. *Private Lives, Public Policy: 100 Years of State Intervention in the Family*. Toronto: Women's Press.

Waldman, A. 2009. *Bad Mother: A Chronicle of Maternal Crimes, Minor Calamities, and Occasional Moments of Grace*. New York: Doubleday Press.

Walker, A. 1973. "Everyday Use" in Walker, A. (Ed.), *In Love and Trouble: Stories of Black Women*. (47–59) Florida: Harcourt Books.

Wallace, M. 1978. *Black Macho and The Myth Of The Superwoman*. The Dial Press.

Waring, W. 1994. "She Tells You Her Story: A Turning Kaleidoscope" in Waring, W. (Ed.), *By, For & About: Feminist Cultural Politics*. (9–24). Toronto: Women's Press.

Wearing, B. 1984. *The Ideology of Motherhood: A Study of Sydney Suburban Mothers*. Sydney, George, Allen & Unwin.

Wells, J. (Ed.). 1997. *Lesbians Raising Sons*. New York: Alyson books.

Witterick, K. 2011. Baby Storms Mom On Gender, Parenting And The Media. <www.vancouversun.com/news/canada/Baby+Storm+gender+parenting+media/4856804/story.html>. Accessed 06/18/2011.

Wolfe, N. 2001. *Misconceptions: Truth, Lies and the Unexpected on the Journey to Motherhood*. New York: Doubleday.

Wong-Wylie, G. Matroreform. *Encyclopedia of Motherhood*. 2010. SAGE

Wong-Wylie, G. 2006. Images and Echoes in Matroreform: A Cultural Feminist Perspective. *Journal for the Association for Research on Mothering* 8 (1&2):135–146.

Wong-Wylie, G. & Russell-Mayhew, S. 2010. "No 'Body" To Blame?: Sociocultural Influences On Girls And Women" in Ross, L. (Ed.), *Counselling Women: Feminist Issues, Theory and Practice*. (195–219). Canadian Scholars' Press/Women's Press.

Young, L. & Cross, W. 2003. "Women and Conservative Parties in Canada and the United States" in Schultze, R-O, Sturm, R., and Eberle, D. (Eds.), *Conservative Parties and Right Wing Politics in North America: Mapping the Benefits of an Ideological Victory?* (207–228). Druck: DruckPartner Rubelmann, Hemsbach, Germany.

INDEX